2oo2
THINGS
TO DO
ON A
Date

Other titles by
Cyndi Haynes and Dale Edwards

2002 Romantic Ideas
2002 Ways to Find, Attract and Keep a Mate
2002 Ways to Say "I Love You"

2002
THINGS
TO DO
ON A
Date

From Fun, Sometimes Silly,
Romantic, To The Unique

Cyndi Haynes & *Dale Edwards*

Adams Media Corporation
Holbrook, Massachusetts

Published by
Adams Media Corporation
260 Center Street, Holbrook, MA 02343

ISBN: 1-58062-079-5

Printed in Canada.

J I H G F E D C B

Library of Congress Cataloging-in-Publication Data
Haynes, Cyndi.
2002 things to do on a date / by Cyndi Haynes and Dale Edwards.
p.   cm.
ISBN 1-58062-079-5
1. Dating (Social customs)—Miscellanea. 2. Recreation—Miscellanea.
I. Edwards, Dale. II. Title.
HQ801.H375   1998
646.7'7—dc21   98–26323
                                      CIP

This book is available at quantity discounts for bulk purchases.
For information, call 1-800-872-5627 (in Massachusetts, 781-767-8100).

Visit our home page at http://www.adamsmedia.com

Good Old-Fashioned Romantic Outings

1. Ride through the park after dark in a horse drawn carriage.

2. Kiss good night.

3. Discover an out of the way cafe.

4. Pray together.

5. Enjoy a sunset walk along the beach.

6. Have "your table" at your favorite restaurant.

7. Lend support during a tough time.

8. Hang mistletoe together.

9. Pass love notes in the library.

10. Sneak away for a moonlit swim.

11. Go to a local grove to pick fruit and then go home and cook something wonderful with it.

12. Flirt only with each other.

13. Forget about having a big wedding and just elope.

14. Stop to make a purchase from a street flower vendor.

15. Share a bag of M & M's.

16. Snuggle.

17. Walk arm in arm on a foggy night.

18. Make a list of your favorite songs, then record a tape.

19. Relax with a brandy by the fire.

20. Act lovey-dovey without being embarrassed.

21. Share a box of Godiva Chocolates.

22. Go parking.

23. Steal a kiss while in a corner booth at a restaurant.

Take a Look!

24. Reserve side by side seats on the couch for Super Bowl Sunday.

25. For a panoramic view, climb a look-out tower.

26. Attend a golf tournament at a local club.

27. Catch the World Series on the tube.

28. Suffer through a slide presentation of your date's recent trip.

29. Check out jai alai together.

30. Watch the pleasure boats scurrying about on the river on a hot Saturday afternoon.

31. Fall head over heels about each other at a diving meet.

32. Celebrate the arrival of spring with the Masters.

33. Gather at a sports bar to watch Monday night football.

34. Start the "wave" at a ball game.

35. Get revved up and watch the Indianapolis 500.

36. Play lacrosse.

37. Host a Final Four party and serve a big pot of chili to get the ball rolling.

38. Watch the Tony Awards.

39. Have a fan–tastic time watching NBA basketball.

40. For two minutes of excitement, watch the Kentucky Derby.

REASONS WHY PEOPLE DATE
Companionship.
To meet exciting people.
All of your friends are dating.
The world seems to be made for couples.
Friendship.
To find a spouse.
All of your friends are married.
It's a lot of fun.

Windows on the World

41. Team up to wax your car in the park.

42. Have friends over for a backyard cookout.

43. Shape up and jog together.

44. Sit outside on the deck to enjoy a meal at a marina restaurant.

45. Make s'mores over a campfire.

46. Put the rest of the world on hold and take a leisurely walk through the woods.

47. Go scuba diving to explore the underwater world.

48. Shake the winter doldrums by shopping at a greenhouse.

49. Visit a national park together.

50. Start the day off right with a sunrise picnic.

51. Stroll through a flower market together.

52. Try cross country skiing.

53. On an autumn day, treat yourselves to a covered bridge tour.

54. Enjoy the charm of a small fishing village.

55. Spend a sunny spring afternoon working in the garden.

56. Get away for a jeep ride in the desert.

57. Brighten your view of the world by planting a window box.

58. Wander through a botanical garden.

59. Make discoveries at a planetarium.

60. Try snorkeling.

61. Take a watercolor class together.

62. Spend the entire day whale watching.

63. Enjoy the view of your city from an overlook.

64. Enroll together in an art appreciation class.

65. Stroll through a campground.

66. Worship together at a sunrise service.

67. Make a stained glass window.

68. Explore a nature center.

69. Plant some bulbs in your garden.

70. Saunter along a brook.

71. Develop your creativity in a photography class.

72. Take a cog railroad ride.

73. Discover an all new world at a wildlife preservation.

74. Enjoy the splendor of autumn with a foliage drive.

On the Town

75. Go all out and dine at a five star restaurant.

76. Get lost in the delightful sounds of a symphony concert.

77. Join your friends for an event at a private club.

78. Celebrate a special occasion with a bottle of vintage wine.

79. Enjoy a stage musical.

80. Enrich yourselves at a cathedral service.

81. Dress your best to go to a formal.

82. Drool your way through a ritzy store.

83. Hire a violinist to play during dinner.

84. Rendezvous for a cup of tea at a grand hotel.

85. Have dinner in an elegant dining car.

86. Experience the magic of the opera.

87. Dress formally for a meal at Burger King.

88. Appreciate the grace and beauty of the ballet.

89. Feel the excitement of an opening night at the theater.

90. Ask your date out with a formal invitation.

91. Treat yourselves to a royal afternoon at a polo match.

92. Hobnob at a black tie dinner.

93. Check out the street magicians.

94. Spice up your life by trying Cajun cooking.

95. Meet for an early morning walk.

96. Enjoy an ethnic festival.

97. Join your grandparents for a Friday night at the VFW Post.

98. Attend a Pops concert.

99. Kick off your shoes and enjoy yourselves at a Japanese restaurant.

100. Join a protest march.

101. Meet your parents for a cocktail.

102. Brush up on your knowledge of history by visiting a historical monument.

103. Stop by a marina to enjoy the view.

104. While walking downtown, treat yourselves to a street vendor meal.

105. Experience the excitement of Chinatown.

106. Dress as tourists and ask strangers to take pictures of the two of you all over town.

107. Collect cocktail napkins of places that you have been together.

108. For country dwellers, spend a day in the city.

109. Celebrate with the winners and cry with the losers at an election night party.

110. Try an ethnic food that neither one of you have had before.

111. See the latest museum exhibit.

112. Pick up a carry-out dinner and enjoy it at your favorite spot.

For Night Owls

113. With a telescope, some munchies and a warm blanket, watch for Halley's comet.

114. Attend midnight services together.

115. Go grocery shopping at 3:00 a.m.

116. Cram for an exam.

117. Meet her after "guy's night out."

118. Go fishing together before the sun comes up.

119. After the party, stop for an early breakfast.

120. Window shop after the stores have closed.

121. Visit an all night restaurant during the early morning hours.

122. Stay up to listen for Santa's reindeer.

123. Share a midnight snack at a roadside diner.

124. Host a pajama party for your friends.

125. Hunt for bargains at a midnight madness sale.

126. Stay up to turn back (or forward) your clocks at 2:00 a.m.

127. Night prowl.

128. Wait in line all night together for tickets.

129. Get a compass, drive a convertible, and hunt for UFOs.

To be loved, be lovable.

—*OVID*

---

130. Enjoy a romantic moonlit picnic.

131. Kick off your shoes and wade knee-deep in a lake.

132. For a long date, play a complete game of Monopoly.

Heart to Heart

133. Make a New Year's resolution list together.

134. Share a root beer float by using two straws.

135. Celebrate your good times (don't take them for granted).

136. Hug.

137. Share your thoughts and feelings about life after death.

138. Request "your song" on the radio.

139. Slow dance at a local club.

140. Serenade each other on the ukulele.

141. Help solve a problem by writing a letter to Dear Abby together.

142. Whisper sweet nothings.

143. Read poetry to each other.

144. Share a brief version of your life story.

145. Take a snuggle break during a stressful time.

146. Celebrate Significant Other Day at the end of each month.

147. Pitch in to help each other solve a problem.

148. E-mail each other when you can't be together in person.

Celebrations

149. Celebrate TGIF together.

150. Make new friends at a neighborhood party.

151. Host a "Christmas in July" party.

152. Attend a church social.

153. Address party invitations together for your upcoming bash.

154. Accompany your date to an office party.

155. Celebrate little dating anniversaries, like your:
First kiss
First date
First fight

156. Throw a bon voyage party for your departing friends.

157. Take up swing dancing.

158. Shake things up by taking a bartending class together.

159. Kick off a sporting event with a pregame party.

160. Blow out your birthday candles and make a wish.

161. Entertain country style with a barn dance.

162. Crash a formal party.

163. Shake the winter doldrums by hosting an indoor beach party.

164. Plan a wedding.

165. Make future plans for the two of you by replying to an RSVP.

166. Host a festive birthday party for your favorite historical figure.

167. Go together to a family Memorial Day picnic.

168. Make candy apples to give away for Halloween treats.

Alone Together . . . at Last

169. Capture the taste of a fall festival.

170. Join in the festive spirit at your company Christmas party.

171. Read the Sunday comics together.

172. Meander back roads without any particular destination in mind.

173. Relax yourselves in a hot tub.

174. Share an ice cream sandwich on a hot summer day.

175. Get away for a day trip.

176. Take advantage of a windy March day by sailing model boats on a lake.

177. Play footsies under the dinner table.

178. Celebrate the arrival of spring at an Easter parade.

179. Trot on over to a horse show.

180. Read quietly side by side on the sofa.

181. Daydream the day away together by planning an imaginary vacation.

182. Sightsee in a nearby town.

183. For a backyard feast, grill some steaks.

184. Take a ferryboat ride.

185. Listen and laugh to a comedy recording.

186. Leave your car at home and walk to wherever you're going.

Off the Beaten Track

187. Fruitcake . . . bake it, eat it, throw the remainder away.

188. Cover the floor with newspapers and fingerpaint a masterpiece.

189. Watch a body building contest.

190. Try learning jujitsu.

191. For a change, listen to a foreign rock group.

192. Jump rope together for fitness.

FIRST DATE ETIQUETTE
Dress accordingly.
Consider your date's finances.
Be positive and enthusiastic.
Don't drink too much.
Keep your sense of humor.
Remember that your date has feelings.
Plan the date well.
Don't go to a singles' hangout.
Offer your date suggestions on appropriate attire.
Wear clothes that make you feel comfortable.
Don't go anywhere it is too loud to talk easily.
Consider your date's interests.
Thank the person at the end of the date.

---

193. Engage in a friendly pillow fight.

194. Act silly by impersonating a favorite celebrity.

195. Celebrate Friday the 13th by sharing your superstitions.

196. Have a fire escape picnic.

197. Make a meal entirely out of grocery store samples.

198. Tune in MTV—and join in with a kazoo.

199. Be adventurous and go to an acupuncture clinic.

200. Visit a stockyard.

201. Have a blast on Alamo Day.

202. Flip a coin to decide what to do on your date.

203. Tell your best UFO story (make one up if you must).

204. Go out for a manicure for two.

205. Compare mood rings or other 70s memorabilia.

206. Don't just hang around the house all day; go bungee jumping.

207. Take harmonica lessons together.

208. Explore a spy store.

209. Beware of werewolves during a full moon.

210. Celebrate Dingus Day (the day after Easter).

211. For a hoot, enter a hog calling contest.

212. Get your kicks by learning Tae Kwon Do.

213. Dine at a truck stop.

214. Form a romantic poetry society.

215. Be chauffeured on the waterways in a gondola.

216. Rent a favorite foreign film.

217. Play an April Fool's Day prank.

218. Crash a large family reunion, then eat and run.

219. Hunt for bargains in a pawn shop.

220. Watch professional wrestling on television.

221. Host a gold fish race party.

222. Enjoy Gary Larson's *The Far Side.*

223. Go Hawaiian by hosting a luau.

224. Watch a dog sled race.

225. Play with your pet rocks.

226. When the pace is too slow, pick it up by playing jacks again.

227. Enter a lip sync contest.

228. Watch a belly dancer.

229. Tie dye your t-shirts.

230. Engage yourselves in a competitive marbles match.

231. Be brave and try ski jumping.

232. For a cheap date, make a meal out of happy hour hors d'oeuvres.

233. Play Koosh ball.

234. Play the newest and most popular computer game.

235. Stay on track by watching roller derby.

236. Enjoy the ancient art of bonsai trees.

237. For self-defense and exercise, learn Kung Fu.

238. Head on over to a demolition derby.

239. Host a masquerade dinner for two.

240. Make the scene together at a fraternity or sorority dance.

For Animal Lovers

241. Pick out your favorite pooch at a dog show.

242. Explore the countryside on horseback.

243. Grab your camera and go to the zoo for a great afternoon.

244. Bring home a doggy bag for your pet.

245. Jump at the opportunity to see an equestrian event.

246. Visit a pet shop and let a puppy steal your heart.

247. Look in the classified ads for a free kitten and bring home a new pal.

248. Take your dog for a walk in the park.

249. Introduce your date to your pets.

250. Feed the burnt piece of meat to the dog while the cook isn't looking.

251. Pick out winners together at the horse races.

252. Take a donkey ride along a mountain trail.

Right After Work

253. Meet for a drink after work in an elegant business district bar.

254. Burn a yule log during the holidays.

255. For a quiet evening, go out for a glass of wine and good conversation.

256. Watch an entire mini-series.

257. Splurge on an expensive, unforgettable night out.

258. When the occasion calls for black tie attire, help him shop for the perfect tuxedo and a fun cummerbund.

Spend more imagination than money.
—*LYNDON B. JOHNSON*

259. Paint the town red together.

260. Host a dinner buffet for your favorite people.

261. Take your chances and throw a casino party.

262. Enjoy the lively atmosphere while dining at a supper club.

263. Relax and get caught up with each other over drinks in a lounge.

264. Host a cocktail party together.

265. To make your date feel special, order dinner for the two of you.

266. Play tennis or racquetball, then enjoy a meal at the club restaurant.

267. Browse an electronic superstore to check out the latest in technology.

268. Celebrate by hosting a birthday dinner.

269. Mingle together at a bierstube—beer garden.

270. Go bowling.

271. Exercise your rights and have an election night party.

272. Enjoy the view from a revolving bar.

At-Home Dates

273. Shop at a second hand store to furnish his bachelor pad.

274. Spread a blanket on the living room floor and have an indoor picnic.

275. Stay at home for the date.

276. For backyard fun, build a deck together.

277. Spend a Sunday afternoon touring the Parade of Homes.

278. Pop popcorn without using a microwave oven.

279. Steady your hands and build a house of cards.

280. Raid the refrigerator.

281. Build an unusual birdhouse and make friends with some feathered creatures.

282. Host a "we finally completed the . . ." party.

283. Lighten the load and help clean the house.

284. Close the curtains and play with an old set of tinkertoys.

285. Enjoy the charm of a historical house tour.

286. Throw a welcome home party for a pal.

287. Go ape and build a tree house.

288. If you like leftovers, have a casserole night at home.

289. Go "house hunting" by looking through the real estate pages.

290. Try your hand at stenciling.

291. Invite your friends to a house painting party.

Improving Yourself, Improving the World

292. Support the candidate of your choice by attending a political rally.

293. Quit smoking for a whole day (and get moral support as you do).

294. Keep up with currents events by watching the local and national news together.

295. Solve a problem with role playing.

296. Watch your government at work during a city council meeting.

297. Teach a Sunday school class together.

298. Philosophize the day away.

299. Enrich yourselves at a Maundy Thursday service.

300. Examine the treasures at a local museum.

301. Take an IQ test.

302. Start your pup off on the right paw and take him to an obedience class together.

303. Have your cholesterol levels checked.

304. Help out by volunteering for a public broadcasting fundraiser.

305. Visit your congressman's local office.

306. Improve yourselves with an image consultant.

307. Learn the facts about AIDS prevention.

308. Critique the play or film you have just seen over a late dinner.

309. Look to the future by joining an investment club.

310. Spend an entire evening counting your blessings.

311. Learn to be dynamic speakers at a Toastmaster's meeting.

312. Go to a biofeedback seminar.

313. Attend a news conference.

314. Critique the newest best-sellers.

315. Visit your city's visitor's bureau to discover something different to do.

316. Stay informed by attending a political speech.

317. Team up for volunteer church work.

318. Donate blood.

319. Rescue a puppy from the pound.

320. For added pocket change, recycle aluminum cans.

321. Support Big Brothers & Sisters.

322. Work on a project to save an animal on the endangered species list.

323. Help the homeless by volunteering at a shelter.

324. Buy raffle tickets to support a good cause.

325. Improve your neighborhood by picking up litter.

WHERE CAN YOU MEET WOMEN?

Coed hair salon	Education center
Craft fair	Cafe
Library	Church
On vacation	Workshop

---

326. Make a list of ten ways that the two of you can improve our planet.

327. Do charity work and feel good about helping others.

328. Volunteer to assist the Special Olympics.

329. Give a little of your time to help the elderly at a local nursing home.

330. Support a Humane Society event.

331. Volunteer to help at a soup kitchen.

332. Team up and write to a serviceman or service woman overseas.

333. Stop by to brighten the day of someone in a nursing home.

334. Adopt your own long-term clean-up spot.

335. Shovel snow for a senior citizen.

336. Recycle newspapers together.

337. Teach a child to read.

338. Celebrate Earth Day by improving our environment.

339. Join a worthwhile boycott.

340. Send a cow to Ethiopia (Heifer Project).

341. Branch out from your routine by planting a tree.

Dancing the Night Away

342. Teach each other to dance.

343. When you're too tired to be up on your feet, try finger dancing.

344. Start with the basics and learn the two step.

345. For fun and romance, go to a dance theater.

346. Attend a country club dance.

347. Pull out your old disco records and do the "Hustle."

348. Catch up with old friends at a homecoming dance.

349. Fast dance at a local hot spot.

350. Kick up your heels and join a dance club together.

351. Display your talents by entering a dance contest.

352. Make new friends at a cotillion.

353. Attend a dance recital.

354. Fox-trot all night long.

355. Dress up and ballroom dance at home by candlelight.

356. Invent a new dance.

357. Watch a tap dancer perform.

358. Go flamenco dancing.

MEETING SOMEONE NEW
Don't surround yourself by so many friends that you
aren't easy to approach.
Smile, be friendly and initiate eye contact.
Host a get-together and invite that person.

I Only Have Eyes for You

359. Celebrate Sweetest Day in October.

360. Read old cards and letters from each other to each other.

361. Help your date select new eyeglass frames.

362. Talk about your previous relationships.

363. Model your new clothes to get your date's opinion.

364. Write poems for each other.

365. Steal a kiss while under the mistletoe.

366. Play hide and seek.

367. Ring in the new year with a romantic New Year's Eve party for two.

368. Cuddle while dancing cheek to cheek.

369. Attend a beauty pageant together.

370. Ask him to a Sadie Hawkins dance.

371. Drift off as you gaze into each other's eyes.

372. Buy matching funky sunglasses.

For Music Lovers Only

373. Get lost in the sounds of a violin concerto.

374. Take guitar lessons together.

375. Sing *Auld Lang Syne* at midnight.

376. For Nashville style fun, watch the Grand Ole Opry.

377. Play "name that tune."

378. Sing along at a gospel concert.

379. Go shopping for stereo equipment (or pretend to).

380. For a very relaxing evening, listen to chamber music.

381. Hit the trail to a Country & Western bar.

382. Spend an evening listening to your ten favorite albums (half the fun is choosing).

383. Drink in the soothing atmosphere of a jazz club.

384. Display your talents by joining a glee club.

385. Have fun hooking up a new stereo system.

386. Listen to a religious radio station.

387. Discuss your musical likes and dislikes.

388. Audition a DJ for your party.

389. Go singing in the rain.

390. Escape to another world at *Madame Butterfly* (opera).

391. Play a duet.

392. Shake your winter doldrums by listening to the sound of the ocean in seashells.

Weekend Winners

393. For absolutely no reason at all, throw a party.

394. Catch a frisbee tournament.

395. Spend a Saturday morning searching for garage sales.

396. Join some friends for a day of boating.

397. Team up to play in a couples' golf tournament.

398. Love strawberries and cream and Wimbledon.

399. Enjoy watching little league baseball.

400. Watch the Muscular Dystrophy Telethon all the way through (and pledge).

401. Explore a street fair together.

402. Try adventure dining—look in the yellow pages to discover a new restaurant and then go.

403. Play boccie ball.

404. Help each other find that perfect gift.

405. Watch a Sunday afternoon rugby match in the park.

406. Host an indoor beach party during the winter.

407. Put on your best poker face for a battle of five card draw.

408. Relax at a coffee house.

409. Experience spiritual growth at a religious retreat.

410. Count the cars on the freeway when you are feeling impatient.

COMMON DATING MISTAKES
Trying too hard.
Not bringing enough cash.
Not making plans.
Holding unrealistic expectations.
Being too rigid.
Leaving your sense of humor at home.
Trying to make an old flame jealous.
Making the date last too long.

---

411. Go for a drive and kiss during red lights.

412. Work on a dude ranch for a day.

413. Have a ball at a tailgate party.

414. Get your kicks by taking a class to learn Karate.

415. Sit side by side on a park bench and watch the world go by.

416. Start a beer can collection.

417. Cheer your friends on at a powderpuff football game.

418. Play a game of tennis.

419. Splish splash at a water park.

420. Try aerobics together.

421. Reach new depths in your relationship—visit a bargain basement.

422. Join a sports car club together.

It's Better to Give Than Receive

423. Pick out a name for your dog.

424. Celebrate Mother's Day by taking your moms out to lunch together.

425. Attend a celebrity auction.

426. Hunt for an anniversary gift for a special couple.

427. Round up your friends for a wild west party.

428. For your friends tying the knot, browse the mall for a wedding present.

429. Spend a Saturday afternoon shopping for Christmas gifts.

430. Shop together for that meaningful christening, birthday, or bar mitzvah gift.

431. Give your own lie detector test.

432. Team up to throw a surprise party for a friend.

433. Have fun shopping together for a special baby gift.

434. Do a good deed by signing up to be organ donors.

435. Put your heads together to come up with ideas for a unique graduation gift.

436. Host an around the world party.

437. Help find that "just right" Father's Day gift.

438. Pitch in together to buy a birthday gift for a mutual friend.

439. Help each other clean out closets and choose which items to give to the Salvation Army.

All Dressed Up

440. Be Romeo & Juliet at a "great couples" costume party.

441. Meet for a drink in an elegant piano bar.

442. Take modeling lessons together.

443. Watch an old situation comedy and make fun of the clothing.

444. Buy matching t-shirts.

445. Help her pick out an Easter bonnet.

446. For that special look, try shopping at a vintage clothing store.

447. Dress as cowpokes and go to a saloon.

448. Attempt to walk in snowshoes.

449. Give yourselves a boost by attending a midweek church service.

450. Offer each other fashion advice.

451. Have a bum night—jeans, t-shirts and spend no more than five dollars.

452. Host an elegant derby party, complete with mint juleps.

453. Check out the new trends at a fashion show.

454. Enjoy a romantic dinner dance aboard a paddle wheeler.

455. Hobnob at a country club brunch.

456. Buy something fun and outrageous at a flea market and wear it during your next date together.

Oldies but Goodies

457. Listen to a golden oldies station.

458. Play a game of hearts—the only romantic card game.

459. Try to improve your game by watching the U.S. Open.

460. Have a drink at a riverboat bar.

461. In your spare time, go miniature bowling.

462. Go to the hair stylist together for new "dos."

463. Shoot baskets.

464. Discover the bargain of a lifetime at a condo auction.

465. For a honey of a date, try beekeeping.

466. Go to a part of town you've never visited.

467. After a trip, greet your date at the airport with a welcome home sign.

468. Decorate your house for autumn by making a scarecrow.

469. Attend a piano recital.

470. Get into shape by working out together to an exercise video.

471. Unwind together in a whirlpool.

472. Trot yourselves over to a harness race.

Women fall in love through their ears and men through their eyes.

—WOODROW WYATT

---

473. Take a class to learn a foreign language together.

474. Participate in a television auction.

475. Try a different kind of kiss—share a bag of Hershey Kisses.

476. Build a ship in a bottle.

477. For breakfast anytime, have a meal at a pancake house.

478. Join in the festivities of a ribbon-cutting ceremony.

479. Enter a radio call-in contest together.

480. Be prepared by earning your lifesaving certificates together.

481. Feel patriotic while watching the Olympic games.

TO BE SUCCESSFUL AT THE DATING GAME ...
Promptly return all phone calls.
Don't play games.
Be fun.
Keep your word.
Learn to be a good host/hostess.
Use good grammar.
Learn to bring out the best in others.
Be adept at meeting people.
Don't lose touch with your friends.
Be willing to get out in the dating world.
Have friends of both sexes.
Go places where singles go.
Don't be a couch potato.
Use good manners.
Be involved in your community.

---

482. Give your date a tote ride on your bike.

483. Capture your favorite spot on canvas with your own oil paintings.

484. Search for hidden treasures with an old map.

485. Be brave and take high diving lessons.

486. Enjoy the fresh air of a springtime lawn party.

487. Tell each other the gory details of your job.

488. Celebrate May Day by giving a beautiful spring bouquet.

489. Send a letter to the president.

490. See who can create the best culinary masterpiece at a salad bar restaurant.

491. Sightsee by car in your city.

492. Take a personality test.

493. Escape your day to day hassles by playing the game of Life.

494. Join a debate team together.

495. Dine on crepes while watching the French Open.

496. Campaign for your favorite candidate.

497. Revive yourselves at a revival.

498. Tour a college campus.

499. Watch a gymnastics meet.

500. Be clowns at a children's hospital.

501. Experience a fine meal at a German restaurant.

Hail, Hail, the Gang's All Here

502. Gather with friends to watch baseball's All-Star game.

503. Host an anniversary party for your folks.

504. Pass the afternoon playing touch football.

505. Suffer together through a family reunion.

506. Invite your friends over for a cocktail.

507. Host a Saturday brunch.

508. Recruit your pals to help support your favorite charity.

509. Mingle through the crowd at a fraternity party.

510. Make nachos for the gang.

511. Pick up a keg of beer and have your friends drop by for an impromptu party.

512. Take your pets along for a day at the beach.

513. Throw a BYOD (donation) bash to support a worthy cause.

514. Team up as partners to play Euchre.

515. Host a cocktail buffet.

516. Eliminate having to decorate for your party by renting the entire museum.

517. Put in an appearance together at a friend's party.

518. When your gang has outgrown your living room, have a garage party.

If You Don't Know All That There Is to Know . . .

519. Prepare for your financial future by enrolling in an investment class together.

520. Hold a Bible study group.

521. Find strange words in the dictionary and bluff each other by coming up with fantasy definitions.

522. Take a foreign language class together.

523. Relax at a stress management seminar.

524. Take a correspondence course together.

525. Improve your frame of mind by listening to a motivational tape.

526. Learn to keep score in the program at a baseball game.

527. Keep up with the times by taking a computer class.

528. Discover more about yourselves with the results from an aptitude test.

529. Take voice lessons together.

530. Learn to oil paint.

531. Read and be amazed with the *Guinness Book of Records*.

532. Be comfortable at a Dale Carnegie training class.

533. Learn to drive a standard shift car.

534. Enroll in a class together at the YMCA.

In the Old Days, You Might . . .

535. Spend a Saturday afternoon making homemade ice cream.

536. Go to your county fair.

537. Listen to classical music.

538. Bake a pie together.

539. Learn to waltz.

540. Refresh yourselves with fresh squeezed lemonade.

541. Snuggle on a hayride.

542. Harvest your garden and can the fresh vegetables.

543. Make your own Christmas ornaments.

544. Join a square-dance club.

545. Watch a silent film and enjoy talking through a movie for a change.

546. Roast marshmallows over the fire.

547. Throw horseshoes.

548. Cruise down the river aboard a paddle wheeler.

549. Try your hand at wood carving.

550. Make homemade jam together to give away as a special gift.

551. Explore a spooky ghost town.

552. Listen to folk music to learn of local lore.

553. After a summertime rainstorm, make mud pies.

554. Watch a bicycle race.

555. Discuss the differences between the sexes.

556. Have a box-lunch date.

557. Roller skate.

558. Share the shade under an oak tree on a hot summer day.

559. Stroll a fairground.

560. Hunt for goodies at a bake sale.

561. Host a Memorial Day picnic for your neighborhood.

562. Compete at card games.

563. Snuggle during a sleigh ride to grandmother's house.

564. Enter your best leaper in a frog race.

565. Enjoy a Coke on the front porch.

566. After the movie, stop for a milkshake.

567. Have fun at a sweet sixteen birthday party.

568. String popcorn for the Christmas tree.

569. Throw an old fashioned hoedown.

570. Take turns on a tire swing.

571. Go strawberry picking.

572. Enjoy the beauty of church bells at Christmastime.

Courting in Style

573. Prepare an elaborate gourmet meal together.

574. Hire an accordion player to entertain during dinner.

575. Read the collected works of Elizabeth Barrett Browning.

576. Impress your date by ordering the meal in a foreign language.

577. Float away on a hot air balloon.

578. Dress up for an evening at home.

579. Sip hot cider with cinnamon by the fire.

580. Drink in the fresh air while dining on the patio.

581. Have a friend chauffeur you and your date around for the evening.

582. Reserve a private dining room for a dinner for two.

583. Celebrate with Dom Perignon.

584. Spend the entire evening savoring a seven-course meal at an elegant restaurant.

585. Enjoy the magic of a candlelight picnic.

586. Toast each other with soft drinks in champagne flutes.

587. Read Emily Post together to improve your manners.

588. Delight in the ambience of a French restaurant.

Sportsman's Choice

589. Go deep-sea fishing for a whale of a time.

590. For an adventurous day of exercising, go mountain biking.

591. Experience the exhilaration of white water rafting.

592. Visit a stable (but watch where you step).

593. Be a pair of early birds when shopping for supplies at a bait and tackle store.

594. Fish for compliments.

595. If you are tired of the ups and downs of everyday life, try rappelling down the sheer face of a cliff.

596. Take riding lessons together.

597. Hunt for a buried treasure.

598. Introduce your date to snipe hunting.

599. Relax on an inner tube float.

600. For a guaranteed lift, join a ski club together.

601. Get out and enjoy the fresh air while mountain climbing.

602. Be prepared and buy your fishing licenses.

603. Browse a sporting goods store.

PEOPLE WHO MIGHT INTRODUCE YOU TO AVAILABLE SINGLES

Co-workers	Neighbors
Minister	Friends
Siblings	Aunts/Uncles
High school friends	College chums
Doctors	Sorority/Fraternity pals

School Bells

604. Attend your high school reunion together.

605. Lend a hand to help address graduation announcements.

606. Watch your favorite college sports team in action.

607. Work on a term paper together.

608. To help ease the tension, go to a finals week party.

609. Visit your old school playground.

610. Get fired up and go to a pep rally.

611. Check out several colleges while trying to decide which one is right for you.

612. Celebrate Class Day together.

613. Team up to work on a school project.

614. Shop for supplies at a back to school sale.

615. Browse the bookstore together.

616. Eliminate the decision of what to wear by throwing a toga party.

617. Participate together in coed intramural sports.

618. Join in the celebration of a graduation party.

619. Get involved by attending a PTA function.

620. Talk about your day at school.

621. Discover an out-of-the-way spot for a campus picnic.

622. Wear your old letter sweater and go to a high school sporting event.

623. See a college play together.

624. Check out a College Union happening.

625. Attend a high school graduation ceremony.

Getting to Know You

626. Take the phone off the hook and chat without interruption.

627. Share your personal beliefs.

628. Offer a shoulder to lean on during a difficult time.

629. Give the grand tour of your work place.

630. Talk about your childhood heroes and heroines.

631. Play the "what if" game and be careful how you answer the questions.

632. Clean up your act by doing your laundry together.

633. Watch home movies.

634. Show off your collections and treasured mementos.

635. Compare fortune cookies.

636. Look through family photo albums.

637. Learn about each other's character by playing the game of Scruples.

638. Talk about your favorite hobbies.

639. Reveal your "most embarrassing" story.

640. Play the game of 20 questions.

641. Share some of your secrets.

642. Read *The Book of Questions* by Gregory Stock, Ph.D.

Our Parents Used to . . .

643. Take a Sunday afternoon drive.

644. Play checkers.

645. Play cribbage.

646. Stroll through a formal garden.

---

*HOW TO TELL IF YOUR RELATIONSHIP
IS ON THE DOWNHILL CURVE
You don't look forward to seeing each other anymore.
You are bored on dates.
You feel stifled.
Your friends tell you to move on with your life.
You no longer look for reasons to call.
You feel that you need more time apart.
A date seems to last forever.
You'd rather be home alone than with your date.
Little things about the other person are
starting to bug you in a big way.*

---

647. Spend the day at a carnival.

648. Walk her home after school and carry her books.

649. To satisfy your sweet tooth, make candy.

650. Play croquet on the front lawn.

651. Host a hillbilly party.

652. Relax at a Labor Day picnic.

653. Jitterbug the night away.

654. Dress up in fabulous costumes for a Halloween party.

655. Play shuffleboard.

656. After church, enjoy a fried chicken dinner.

657. Stroll through the midway at a fair.

658. Order a cherry cola with two straws.

659. For a date that's right on target, play darts.

660. Make a paper garland for the Christmas tree.

661. Play Parcheesi.

662. Listen to your echoes in a cave.

663. Do the twist.

664. Ride around town in a streetcar.

665. Enjoy a Sunday afternoon double feature.

666. Play bridge.

667. Strike out of your regular routine and go to a minor league baseball game.

668. Keep your fingers crossed for a white Christmas.

669. Have a coffee date.

Time Marches On

670. Run in a marathon race together.

671. Tour a historic log cabin.

672. Start the year off right by attending a New Year's Day party.

673. Return those overdue library books .

674. Pow-Wow at an Indian reservation.

675. Beachcomb together.

676. Attend a Civil War reenactment.

677. Stroll along the boardwalk hand in hand.

678. Go see a marching band.

679. Be lazy together.

680. Get away from the rat race by visiting a colonial village recreation.

681. Team up to throw a graduation party.

682. Play fish.

683. Celebrate the shortest day of the year: December 21st.

684. For an endurance date, enter a dance marathon contest.

685. Capture days gone by at a historical park.

686. Co-host a retirement party for a special friend.

687. Learn to dance the Charleston.

The Best Things in Life Are Free

688. Run barefoot through the park.

689. Watch the last ember in the fireplace go out.

690. Wander the heavens while looking through a telescope at the stars.

691. Wade knee-deep in a fountain.

692. Dance at home to the radio.

693. Watch future superstars at a little league football game.

694. Bathe your dog together.

695. Bundle up and build a snowman.

696. Turn off all the room lighting and capture the quiet splendor of a lit Christmas tree.

697. Try snow painting.

698. Relax at a Sunday afternoon concert in the park.

699. Worship together at a small country church.

700. Go horseback riding on the beach.

701. Skate without skates after an ice storm.

Love does not consist in gazing at each other but in looking together in the same direction.

—ANTOINE DE SAINT-EXUPERY

---

702. People watch at the mall.

703. Cheer at a local youth soccer game.

704. Catch some rays together.

705. With lawn chairs in hand, go early to get a good spot to enjoy a local parade.

706. Sing together in the local choir.

707. Spend a spring afternoon bird watching.

708. Make snow ice cream.

The More the Merrier

709. Attend your company picnic and show off your date.

710. Warm up with a chili dinner on a cold night.

711. Throw a BYOB/BYOG party (old boyfriends & girlfriends) to introduce your single friends to each other.

712. Accompany your date to a reception.

713. Join the fun at your niece or nephew's first birthday party.

714. Enjoy a 50th wedding anniversary celebration.

715. Host a wine tasting party.

716. For a bow-wow bonanza, throw a birthday party for your dog.

717. Dress warmly for a winter party on the beach.

718. Plan your guest list for a joint party.

719. Play charades.

720. Mingle together at an office party.

721. Celebrate the birthday of a friend.

722. Share in the excitement of an engagement announcement party.

723. Put in an appearance at a relative's open house.

724. With steady hands, stack dominoes.

725. Begorrah, why not host a St. Patrick's Day party?

The Most Wonderful Time of the Year

726. Spend a delightful evening decorating the Christmas tree.

727. Celebrate winter break together.

728. Get into the holiday spirit by listening to Christmas music.

729. Feel the excitement and joy of an old-fashioned holiday meal.

730. Dream of fabulous gifts under your tree as you window shop at Christmastime.

731. Prepare a holiday feast together.

732. Share your memories of past holidays.

733. Celebrate New Year's Eve at home together.

734. Get together with good friends for a special Christmas party.

735. Go panic shopping together on December 24th.

736. Enjoy a picnic in the snow with candles, hot chocolate and your date to keep you warm.

737. Kick up your heels at a spring dance.

738. Watch *A Christmas Carol* to catch the spirit of the holidays.

739. Spend a fall afternoon raking leaves together.

740. Select a Christmas tree and try not to get one that looks like Charlie Brown's.

741. Eat sauerkraut on New Year's Day for good luck.

COMPONENTS OF A QUALITY RELATIONSHIP

Worship together	*Commitment*
Honesty	*Consideration*
Loyalty	*Courtesy*
Compassion	*Esteem*
Friendship	*Sincerity*
Love	*Affection*
Sensitivity	*Tenderness*
A sense of fun	*Mutual interests*
Understanding	*Compatibility*
Admiration	*Devotion*
Respect	*Harmony*
Trust	*Laughter*
Faith in each other	*Generosity*

---

742. Fight the crowds together the day after Thanksgiving (the busiest day of the year).

743. Make Easter baskets for underprivileged kids.

744. Share egg nog by the tree.

745. Go to a Christmas tree show to gather ideas on how to decorate your tree.

746. Watch the parades together on Thanksgiving Day.

747. Browse a Christmas store to find that special ornament.

748. Spend a snow day together.

749. See *The Nutcracker Suite* at Christmastime.

750. Dress in festive evening clothing to attend a holiday dance.

751. Take down your Christmas tree together to make what would have been a sad occasion a fun one.

Surf's Up

752. Set sail on a rented pontoon boat.

753. Grab a bite to eat while poolside.

754. Go to a seafood restaurant and select your own lobster for dinner.

755. On a hot day, push your date into the pool (then run).

756. Experience the exhilaration of speedboating.

757. Take off for a day cruise.

758. Enjoy a picnic at the beach.

759. Go swimming on New Year's Day with the Polar Bear Club.

760. Search for pearls in oysters.

761. Browse a boat show.

762. Body surf.

763. Dine at a seaside restaurant.

764. Hang ten while surfing.

765. Sand, sun, friends, food and drink—the ingredients for a super beach party.

766. Have a water balloon fight.

767. Keep cool while sunbathing in a baby pool.

768. Charter a boat for an aquatic adventure.

769. Spend the afternoon at a river camp.

770. Discover a picturesque spot at the lake and etch.

771. Visit a lighthouse on a foggy night.

772. Go exploring in a glass bottom boat.

773. For your "seafood lover" friends, host a clambake.

774. Jump into the fun at your neighborhood pool.

775. Be entertained with the show at a water theme park.

776. Take swimming lesson together.

777. Volunteer at a camp for inner city kids.

It Takes Two

778. Play racquetball for a good work out.

779. Split a banana split.

780. Team up to entertain together.

781. Enjoy an autumn day paddle boating.

782. Learn to play chess.

783. Even at the risk of getting egg on your face, enter an egg toss contest.

784. Share a hymnal.

785. Role play to prepare for a job interview.

786. Try fencing.

787. Practice for a kissing marathon.

788. Play table shuffleboard.

789. Engage in a battle of laser tag.

790. Give piggy back rides.

791. Share an umbrella during a thunderstorm.

792. Play ping-pong.

793. Prevent sunburn—put suntan lotion on each other.

794. Play pitch & catch in the backyard.

795. Snap photos of each other .

796. Play football.

797. Frame a picture together at a frame-it-yourself shop.

798. Play double solitaire (without cheating).

799. Enjoy an afternoon of backgammon.

800. Don't waste food, share a Chinese meal.

801. Teeter-totter an evening away.

802. To prevent chapped lips, try Eskimo kissing.

803. Enjoy Chateaubriand for two.

804. Play air hockey.

Getting Back to Nature

805. Explore an unknown path through the woods.

806. Take a portable grill to the park and fix a fun feast.

807. Dodge raindrops together.

808. Break through your winter routine by ice fishing.

809. Spend a day on a farm.

DATING IN THE WORK PLACE
Check office policy.
Use discretion.
Be prepared for office gossip.
Avoid PDA (Public Display of Affection).
Examine your own motives for dating this person.
Consider whether your career will
suffer if the relationship ends.

---

810. Celebrate the arrival of spring by hosting a garden party.

811. Play in a summer rain shower.

812. Take a stroll through the woods to pick wild flowers.

813. Warm your fingers and toes at a winter wiener roast.

814. Enjoy the quiet beauty of a sunrise.

815. See how many times that you can make a rock skip across a pond.

816. Plant next year's Christmas tree.

817. Chase butterflies.

818. Rejuvenate yourselves at a mineral spring.

819. Try rock collecting (we recommend diamonds).

820. Run barefoot on the beach.

821. If you live in the city, spend an entire day in the country.

822. Explore a national forest.

823. Sneak away for an outdoor nap.

824. Gather pine cones for your Christmas decorations.

825. Enjoy hiking for the exercise and fresh air.

826. Dig up night crawlers for fishing bait.

827. Spend an afternoon picking wild mushrooms.

828. Team up to chaperone a youth group camp out.

There's Magic in the Air

829. Ask your date out in a spectacular way by hiring a skywriter.

830. Every 76 years, host a Halley's Comet party.

831. Leave the hustle and bustle behind and float away in a glider.

832. Let your minds soar while watching a balloon race.

833. Arrive in time for a farewell drink at an airport private club.

834. Soar off to an aviation show.

835. Chase rainbows together.

836. Pack a cooler and take lawn chairs along to watch a volcano erupt.

837. Get up the nerve to try skydiving.

838. Take a helicopter ride and enjoy the view.

839. Catch some rays on the roof of a skyscraper.

840. Admit your relationship fears to one another.

841. Set the mood by burning incense.

842. Wish upon a shooting star.

843. Let your minds wander off as you star gaze together.

FIRST DATE SAFETY
Meet at a neutral location.
Always have your own transportation.
Pick a place to meet with which you are familiar.
Meet in a public spot that is well lighted.
Let a friend know where you are and
when you will be home.

---

844. Act crazy by riding up and down in a glass elevator several times while enjoying the view.

845. Go plane watching at the airport late at night.

846. Enter a kite flying contest.

847. Entertain your friends at a rooftop party.

848. Challenge each other to a watermelon seed spitting contest.

849. Lie on your back and pick out cloud formations.

850. To avoid the risk of blindness, keep your eyes closed and kiss during a solar eclipse.

851. Be amazed at a magic show.

Communication Is the Key

852. Attend a writing workshop together.

853. Phone date.

854. Talk in a foreign language for the entire date.

855. Go to a prayer meeting.

856. Learn Braille together.

857. Give hints about what you want for Christmas.

858. Give hints about the Christmas gifts that you've bought.

859. Complete a self-help magazine questionnaire.

860. Be a good sport and listen to your date practice their speech.

861. Take a sign language class together.

862. Team up to create doodle art.

863. Start the weekend early by going out for lunch on Friday and playing hooky for the rest of the day.

864. Write a letter to your congressman.

865. Dazzle your date with your knowledge of trivia.

866. Take a calligraphy class.

867. Teach a bird to talk.

Cozy Corner

868. Warm up with hot cocoa and a blanket on a cold night.

869. Discover a quaint country cafe.

870. Share a lazy Sunday evening on the porch swing.

871. Read a good mystery novel together and solve it.

872. Build a gingerbread house.

873. Take a break from a hectic day to enjoy a private picnic in your office.

874. Sip an after dinner liqueur.

875. Savor quiet time together after a long and busy day.

876. Hang Christmas stockings with care.

877. Be couch potatoes together.

878. Spend a morning browsing through magazines at a newsstand.

879. Curl up together next to a window and watch it snow.

880. Host a small intimate dinner party.

881. The perfect snack—hot cocoa and animal crackers on a winter evening.

882. Share part of yourself during a fireside chat.

883. Orchestrate a coffee break from work together.

The Couple that Plays Together
Stays Together

884. Join a coed volleyball league.

885. Play Putt-Putt golf.

886. Have a snowball fight.

887. Perform your best card tricks and then share the secret of how it is done.

The best gifts are tied with heartstrings.

—Anonymous

---

888. Head for the slopes to do some skiing.

889. Compete at gin rummy.

890. Learn to play paddleball.

891. Be co-owners in a fantasy sports league.

892. Challenge each other at Nintendo.

893. Play on a coed softball team.

894. Chill out together on a hot summer day by going swimming.

895. Build a snow fort.

896. Risk your fortunes at penny-ante poker.

897. Learn to play squash.

898. Try your hand at handball.

899. Frolic at the bottom of a waterfall.

900. Join a mixed bowling league.

901. Play tic-tac-toe to determine who will pay for dinner (best two out of three).

The Stuff of Which Dreams Are Made

902. Make your Christmas lists.

903. Tour a local mansion and imagine what your lives would have been like had you lived there.

904. Attend a jewelry auction.

905. Throw coins in a wishing well.

906. Share the fantasy of how you would spend a million dollars in one week.

907. Show off your trophies and awards.

908. Delight in a Neiman Marcus Christmas catalog.

909. Enter a comedy search contest at a night club.

910. Share your life long dreams.

911. Dress up and shop for something that you can't afford.

912. Team up to devise a fabulous money making project.

913. Window shop elegant stores.

914. Check out the new sports cars at an auto show.

915. Nap on a lap.

916. Saunter through a chic boutique.

917. Make a birthday wish list.

918. Share your career goals.

919. Determine how to spend your future lottery winnings (just in case).

920. Beat the rush and go early to pan for gold.

921. Throw coins in a fountain and hope that your dreams will come true.

For the Young at Heart

922. Take a walk in the magical world after a late night snowfall.

923. Host a special birthday party (16th, 21st, 30th . . .).

924. Venture to the park together on a cold night with a thermos of hot chocolate.

925. Kidnap your date from work.

926. Try your hand at snow sculpting.

927. Go trick or treating again.

928. Relax on a riverboat cruise.

929. Spend a carefree day lounging by the pool.

930. Be silly together in a photo booth and capture the fun on film.

931. Buy Cracker Jacks and hunt for the prize.

932. Be brave and try something totally outrageously adventurous.

933. Cooking 101 . . . Slice & Bake cookies.

HOSTING A DINNER DATE

Make something that will allow you to spend time with your date and not the entire time in the kitchen.
Set an attractive table.
Clean your place beforehand.
Allow time before the meal for a drink and conversation.
Make your date feel comfortable in your home.
Cook something that you have had success with in the past.
If the results don't turn out as planned, have a "Plan B" ready.

---

934. Make funny faces at the chimps in the zoo.

935. Go sledding on a Saturday morning.

936. Visit a comic book dealer and be amazed at how expensive your old comics are today.

937. Share a bag of gummy bears.

938. Act like kids again and watch a Disney classic.

939. Show off your yo-yo tricks.

940. Browse an antique toy fair.

941. Build a clubhouse for a little friend.

942. Spend an entire afternoon at the arcade.

943. Challenge each other to a sidewalk tic-tac-toe match.

944. Play crazy eights.

945. Look through your childhood books together and reminisce.

946. Build a model.

947. Visit a petting zoo.

948. Try to get a boomerang to work.

949. Ride the kiddie train around the zoo.

950. After a big fight, create a new beginning in your relationship.

951. Build an intricate dollhouse.

952. Stay up late to watch for Santa.

953. Browse a toy store and relive the wonderful magic of childhood.

954. Watch the Harlem Globetrotters.

955. Compete at video games.

956. Have fun at the circus again.

Birds of a Feather Flock Together

957. Join a bicycle club together and enjoy touring the countryside.

958. Flock to a pet store to buy a bird.

959. Be adventurous and charter a plane.

960. Join the MUFONS (Mutual UFO Networks).

961. Contribute to a worthy cause.

962. Play badminton.

963. Get wild and become involved in your area Wildlife Society.

964. Join fellow believers at a religious organization.

965. When the ground is covered with snow, be a good duck and feed the birds.

966. March off to an American Legion function.

967. Attend the Democratic convention.

968. Attend the Republican convention.

969. Join a social club together to make new friends.

970. Express yourselves by taking part in a march.

971. Be "King and Queen for the Day."

It's Show Time

972. Watch Saturday morning cartoons and share a box of doughnuts.

973. Talk about your favorite television shows and make plans to watch one in the near future.

974. Audition together for a bit part in a movie.

975. Watch the American Music Awards.

976. Tour a local television station.

977. Attend a high school play.

978. Check out the new videos on VH1.

979. Spend the afternoon hooking up your new VCR.

980. Sneak a picnic dinner into a movie theater.

981. Call a radio shrink and get help with your dating dilemma.

982. For a change, attend a variety show.

983. Slide on down to an ice show.

984. Critique the season's new television shows.

985. Watch a street magician perform.

986. Attend a motion picture premiere.

987. Tune into the most romantic show on television and pick up a few love life tips.

988. Avoid having a dog day afternoon by attending a dog show.

989. Host a dress rehearsal party.

990. Read the book *and* see the movie together.

991. Discover future stars at a talent show .

992. Pause for a minute to view a puppet show at the mall.

993. Catch a special event on closed circuit television.

994. Watch the local news to learn of any upcoming events of interest for future dates.

995. Gather with friends to cheer for your team at a bar with a big screen television.

996. Entertain yourselves with HBO.

997. View a one act play.

998. Listen to a motion picture soundtrack.

999. Stay up late to watch David Letterman.

1000. Go to a ballet recital.

1001. Browse through a baseball card show.

1002. Sneak away to a matinee.

1003. Rock to MTV.

1004. Shop for knick-knacks at a craft show.

1005. Watch the taping of a television program.

DATING FACT
Most men are flattered when they are asked out.

1006. Enjoy yourselves at a comedy club.

1007. Take the time to stop and listen to a street musician.

1008. Watch television outside under the stars.

1009. For a long date, watch the Academy Awards.

Around the Town

1010. Have a car phone date when you are both driving home from work.

1011. Go bric a brac hunting at out of the way shops.

1012. Take a harbor tour.

1013. Enjoy a picnic at a scenic spot inside a chauffeured limousine.

1014. Go on a scavenger hunt.

1015. Take a taxi around your city to see the sights.

1016. Ride a double-decker bus.

1017. Put a note in two balloons to see which one goes the farthest (the loser buys lunch when the results land).

1018. Crash a wedding reception.

1019. Spend a summer's night cruising.

1020. Enjoy the coziness of a corner tavern.

1021. Pitch in and help with the chore of packing and moving to a new place.

1022. Shop street vendors for bargains.

1023. Go out to a special restaurant to celebrate your raise.

1024. Enjoy a ride in a convertible on a beautiful spring day.

1025. Tour a historical building.

1026. Shop the downtown area of your city.

1027. Have dinner at a cafeteria.

1028. View the city lights at night from a skyscraper.

1029. Enjoy a meal at an outdoor cafe on a nice evening.

Cash or Charge?

1030. Go on a wild, carefree shopping spree.

1031. Thumb through a Spiegel catalog and share your likes and dislikes.

1032. Hunt for great buys at an outlet mall.

1033. Buy an "Our first Christmas together" ornament.

1034. When you need a unique gift, shop at a novelty store.

1035. Sort through the trash and treasures at a flea market.

1036. Attend an antique show and be amazed by the prices.

1037. Browse a charity shop.

1038. Join in the excitement by placing a bid at an auction.

1039. Try the horseman's favorite stop, go to a tack shop.

1040. Shape up and shop for fitness equipment.

1041. Buy great mementos at a souvenir shop.

1042. Daydream at a boat dealership.

Why Not?

1043. Forget your troubles in a jacuzzi for two.

1044. Get in the spirit and make Christmas decorations.

1045. Host a Friday the 13th party.

1046. Experience the down to earth fun of a mud drag.

1047. Use apples and oranges to learn how to juggle.

1048. Bury your own time capsule of mementos of your relationship.

1049. Start a baseball card collection.

1050. Take a busman's holiday.

1051. Hoof it to a horse auction.

1052. Waterpaint together.

1053. Don't just complain about your city, write a letter to the mayor.

1054. Take off and fly remote controlled planes on a pretty afternoon.

1055. Loosen up with Tai Chi Chaun.

1056. Watch a television crusade.

1057. Meet your friends at a dive bar.

1058. Try your luck and enter a contest.

1059. You won't regret it if you play the game of Sorry.

1060. Enjoy dining at a Chinese restaurant.

1061. Browse another city's newspaper to find something unusual to do.

1062. Join cat lovers at a cat show.

1063. Do something silly enough to get in your local newspaper.

1064. Wrap your fun gifts in the Sunday comics.

1065. Invent something.

1066. Warm up with Irish coffee on a cold evening.

1067. Add to your joint stamp collection.

1068. Try making a cheese fondue on a cold night.

1069. Keep up on local events by attending a public meeting.

1070. Fix flapjacks for a Saturday supper.

1071. With the remote control in hand, channel jump on cable television.

1072. Plan for the future together, buy a savings bond.

1073. Procrastinate the day away.

1074. Talk about your favorite sports.

1075. Try the expressive art of folk dancing.

1076. Watch and bid during a television auction for something for the two of you.

1077. Have your portrait professionally done at a studio.

1078. View the AIDS quilt.

1079. Spice up your life by planting a herb garden.

1080. Learn to rollerblade.

1081. Play computer games.

1082. Stay in shape during the winter by jogging on an indoor track.

1083. Watch an obedience trial for dogs.

1084. Listen to country music.

1085. Celebrate Ground Hog Day by checking for his shadow.

1086. Stop an elevator between floors and have a picnic for two.

1087. Sit on the dock of the bay.

1088. Buy matching BMWs.

1089. Charter a helicopter.

1090. To find something different to do, flip through your city's magazine.

1091. Gallop off to a dressage event.

1092. Throw a Super Bowl party.

1093. Pick out star constellations on a clear winter's night.

1094. Buy copies of this book for all of your friends.

1095. Be a sport and listen to your date's presentation.

1096. Date by the Golden Rule to improve your love life.

1097. Make sugar cookies using fun cookie cutters.

1098. Get back to nature and go mountaineering.

1099. Fly away (pilot's license helpful).

1100. For a change, go to a coin show.

1101. Bebop around town.

1102. Be adventurous and walk along the cliffs.

1103. On a snowy day, escape to a hothouse.

Social Life

1104. Start off your weekend at a Friday night cocktail party.

1105. Double date.

1106. Celebrate Boss's Day by throwing a small party.

1107. Dive into summer by hosting a pool party.

1108. Fellowship at a church supper.

TERRIFIC IDEAS FOR SMALL OR UNEXPECTED GIFTS

This book	*Magazine subscription*
Heart-shaped boxes	*Candy*
A special dessert	*Tickets to an event*
CDs	*Stuffed animals*
Silver bud vase	*Flowers*
Music box	*Photos of you*
Hershey kisses	*T-shirts*
An engraved gift	*Homemade jam*
Novel	*Cologne*
Balloons	*Posters*
New gadget	*A tin of cookies*
Beach towels	*Homemade brownies*
Monogrammed gym bag	*Bookmark*
Home-grown veggies	*A gift for a pet*

1109. Hobnob together at a black tie reception.

1110. Join in the celebration at a Presentation Ball.

1111. Team up to host a New Year's Day breakfast for your family.

1112. Rent out a spa for a party.

1113. After playing 18 holes, meet for lunch at the country club.

1114. Be a sport and suffer through a business dinner.

1115. Support a Junior League function.

1116. Go out to dinner with your parents.

1117. Mingle with your friends at a wedding reception.

1118. Cover all the bases and throw a World Series party.

1119. Go to a family birthday dinner.

Be Prepared

1120. Prepare an earthquake survival kit.

1121. Team up to decorate for your party.

1122. Take a first aid class together.

1123. Pack your picnic basket.

1124. Arrange to have Happy Birthday sung after dinner at a restaurant.

1125. Help prepare the hors d'oeuvres before your guests arrive.

1126. Enroll in a auto repair class together.

1127. Practice your "Boss, I want a raise" speech to one another.

1128. When things heat up, check the batteries in your smoke detector.

1129. Study together.

1130. Read the Sunday ads to plan your bargain shopping.

1131. Assemble a first aid kit.

1132. Don't get all shook up, attend an earthquake preparedness seminar.

1133. Practice your putting in the living room.

1134. Take a self defense class together.

1135. Learn CPR (in case of a broken heart).

Old Favorites

1136. Savor the brief moments of a spectacular sunset.

1137. Take a walk arm in arm in the falling snow.

1138. Talk the afternoon away at an enclosed sidewalk cafe on a rainy day.

1139. Share your feelings by writing a love poem together.

1140. Enjoy McDonalds by candlelight on the living room coffee table.

1141. Follow your heart and your head when you go out on a date.

1142. Share wine from a boda (a Spanish leather drinking pouch).

1143. Order dinner from an expensive restaurant in a distant city and have it flown in.

1144. Start your own traditions.

1145. Make plans for future dates together.

1146. Relax with hot buttered rum by a roaring fire.

1147. Discuss your favorite romantic self-help author's ideas.

1148. Treat yourselves to a catered dinner at home.

1149. When the power fails . . .

1150. Rendezvous in the bathroom at a party for a clandestine kiss.

1151. Host a private girlfriend/boyfriend appreciation party.

1152. Turn off the world and enjoy each other.

1153. *Love Story* . . . read, watch and cry.

DATING FACT
Time proven advice: you can't judge a book by its cover.

Something New

1154. If you love Perry Mason, try the real thing by observing a trial in progress.

1155. To get your heart pumping, go through a haunted house.

1156. Throw a backwards party, where everyone comes dressed with their clothes inside out, walks backwards and speaks in Pig Latin.

1157. Meet for breakfast before work.

1158. Expand your artistic abilities by taking a tole-style painting class.

1159. Do doughnuts in a parking lot after a snowfall.

1160. Rent a tandem bicycle to go exploring.

1161. Tour a docked ship (you can be sure that you won't get seasick).

1162. Color night out—pick a color, then choose a restaurant that is decorated in that color and wear that color and go.

1163. Spend a Saturday afternoon together running errands.

1164. Write the governor to express your concerns.

1165. Fall in line and visit a fort.

1166. Discover the underwater world at an aquarium.

1167. For a new twist of dinner and a movie, make a meal out of the concessions at the theater.

1168. Go to a boxing match.

1169. Get in the spirit and tour a distillery.

1170. A double header date—play two different sports on one date.

1171. Take part in a political function.

1172. Enjoy a walk along a wharf at sunset.

1173. Go motorcycle riding on the back roads.

1174. To find something out of the ordinary, browse a museum shop.

1175. Stroll through an open air market.

1176. Host a "come as you are" party.

1177. Shop a wholesale club for some unusual buys.

1178. Make a jack-o-lantern.

1179. For a taste of Mexico, go out for a margarita.

1180. Rendezvous at a park during your lunch hour for a brown bag meal.

1181. Watch a juggler.

1182. Experience a stockyard auction.

1183. Treat yourselves to a hibachi meal.

1184. For an easygoing afternoon, play Uno.

1185. Launch a pontoon boat party.

1186. Be patriotic by working at the polls.

1187. Wander through a Chinese garden.

1188. Loosen up and enter a limbo contest.

1189. Attend a performance of the opera *La Boheme.*

1190. Try tobogganing.

1191. Tone up by pumping iron.

1192. Discover a secluded beach and savor life away from civilization.

1193. Mellow out at a blues bar.

The Way to the Heart Is Through the Tummy

1194. Enjoy a midnight dinner by candlelight.

1195. Share red licorice strings at the movies.

1196. Have a food fight.

1197. Take a gourmet cooking class together.

1198. Finger paint with pudding.

1199. Select choice meat at a butcher shop for your dinner party.

INSTEAD OF ALWAYS SENDING ROSES . . .

Tulips	*Peonies*
Chocolate roses	*Silk flowers*
Irises	*Violets*
A plant	*Miniature rose bush*
Fresh floral bouquets	*Daisies*

1200. Make a meal from vending machines.

1201. Name all of your favorite foods.

1202. Gather nuts in the fall for holiday decorations.

1203. Visit a patisserie and indulge yourselves.

1204. Make a homemade pizza.

1205. Pick blueberries and then bake a pie.

1206. Bake brownies together, then top with vanilla ice cream, whipped cream and nuts, and then go hog wild.

1207. Create a three-egg omelet masterpiece.

1208. Go on a diet fling—get off your diet for one fabulous meal.

1209. Spoil yourselves with chocolate fondue, fresh fruit & champagne.

1210. Host a backyard barbecue.

1211. Prepare your favorite recipe together.

1212. Treat yourselves to strawberry shortcake.

1213. Devour a box of fudge while watching television.

1214. Sample delectables at a food fair.

The Great Outdoors

1215. Relax while watching a sailboat race.

1216. Walk around your neighborhood to enjoy the Christmas lights.

1217. Marvel at a water show.

1218. Continue the tradition of hiding Easter eggs.

1219. See a summer play at an amphitheater.

1220. Go fly a kite.

1221. Experience a windjammer cruise.

1222. Race to the bottom of a water slide.

1223. Bundle up and go outside to play in the snow.

1224. Enjoy the sunshine while throwing a frisbee in the park.

1225. Wash your hair together in the pouring rain.

1226. Build a fabulous sand castle.

1227. Snuggle up next to a campfire on the beach.

1228. Team up to hunt for a four leaf clover.

1229. Spend a day together at a ranch.

1230. Sit on a riverbank and daydream what your lives will be like ten years from now.

1231. Enjoy a walk in the rain on a summer day.

1232. When all other conversation fails, talk about the weather.

1233. Join your friends at a volleyball party.

1234. Bury each other in fall leaves.

1235. Support the Audubon Society.

1236. Get up and go, after learning how to water ski.

1237. Experience the thrill of inner tubing behind a speedboat.

1238. Branch out and climb a tree.

1239. Gather flowers from your garden.

1240. Host a BYOF (fireworks) extravaganza on Uncle Sam's birthday.

1241. Watch a log rolling contest.

1242. Sneak away for a picnic in the middle of a football field in an empty stadium.

1243. Wander through a nearby state park.

Be Team Players

1244. On the evening of April 14th, help prepare tax forms.

1245. Get away for a Saturday canoe trip.

1246. Share your class notes.

1247. Coach a little league team together.

1248. Pick out and address Christmas cards.

1249. Caddie for your date at a golf tournament.

1250. Make a "create as you go" spaghetti sauce.

1251. Help decorate each other's office.

1252. Dress alike for the day.

1253. Improve your health by starting a cholesterol-lowering diet together.

1254. Taxi your date while their car is in the shop

1255. Help with the dishes.

1256. If you are tired of bouncing all over town, stay at home to balance your checkbooks.

1257. Team up to aid the Red Cross during a disaster.

1258. Sneak away for the day together after calling in sick.

1259. Design a couples' Halloween costume for the two of you.

1260. Try a merger—invest in a penny stock together.

1261. Help prepare a resume.

1262. Have a rummage sale together and use the proceeds to splurge for an expensive night out on the town.

1263. Spend the day parasailing.

1264. Cheer from the sidelines for your date.

1265. Help him shop for clothes.

Places to Go—Things to Do

1266. Browse through an art gallery.

1267. Enjoy a casual supper at a friend's place.

1268. For a day of adventure, go yachting.

One word frees us of all the weight and pain of life: that word is love.

—SOPHOCLES

The cautious suitor who stays on the fence too long usually ends up getting the gate.

—ANONYMOUS

1269. Tour a winery.

1270. Pick out a nearby unknown town on the map and spend the day exploring.

1271. Get lost in a maze.

1272. Experience a Mexican fiesta.

1273. Join the old gang during a homecoming weekend.

1274. Meet for a Sunday brunch.

1275. Go foot stomping at a blue grass festival.

1276. Make an extravagant purchase together.

1277. Have dinner at a diner.

1278. Revive your school spirit at an alumni function.

1279. Treat yourselves to a gourmet picnic.

1280. Avoid salesmen by Sunday afternoon car shopping.

1281. Check out an expo.

1282. Armed with credit cards, go shopping together.

1283. Drift on down to a flatboat race.

1284. Check out a 4-H Club event.

1285. Accompany your date to a school function.

1286. Warm up while shopping at a woolen mill.

1287. Dine at a grill.

1288. Celebrate with your friends at their wedding.

Blast From the Past

1289. Read Shakespeare.

1290. Delight in a Vaudeville show.

1291. Reminisce about your past dates together.

1292. Tour an abandoned mine to search for treasures.

1293. Share childhood memories with each other.

1294. Hula hoop again.

1295. Listen to *Mystery Theater* on the radio.

1296. Explore a ruin.

1297. Restore an antique car together.

1298. Relax on a day long steamship ride.

1299. Enjoy the ambience of a century old bar.

1300. Go fossil hunting.

1301. Dress the part and go to a sock hop.

1302. Share the scale of a weight and fortune machine.

1303. Browse an antique auction.

1304. Entertain together with an afternoon tea party.

1305. Visit a historic battlefield.

1306. Journey to a medieval banquet.

1307. Lift off from your regular routine by launching a model rocket.

1308. Try doing the polka.

1309. Hunt for treasures at a sports memorabilia auction.

1310. Experience a relaxing scenic train ride.

1311. Participate in an archaeological dig.

1312. Share some laughs while looking through your baby pictures.

1313. Hang out and feel groovy at a 60's bar.

1314. Go touring in an antique car.

What Romance Is All About

1315. Dance the night away.

1316. Enjoy a long walk together at sunset.

1317. Dim the lights and listen to Luther Vandross.

1318. Kiss hello every time that you see each other.

1319. Discover the language of love, take a poetry class together.

1320. Discover "your" restaurant.

1321. Bring her flowers and candy.

1322. Get away for a romantic picnic for two.

1323. Charm the socks off each other.

1324. Instead of a blockbuster, go to an epic romantic love story.

1325. Watch the submarine races.

1326. Dance the tango, the most romantic dance.

1327. Leave the party early so the two of you can spend some time alone.

1328. Celebrate your relationship with an elegant dinner using fine china and crystal.

1329. Sit back and watch the fog roll in over the lake.

1330. Take a quiet moonlit walk.

1331. Share an elegant dinner aboard your yacht (a rented row boat will do).

Tried and True

1332. Stay at home and order a Domino's Pizza.

1333. Go to a concert.

1334. If you need a break, shoot pool.

TOWARD A BETTER RELATIONSHIP
Maintain open communication.
Use tact.
Make a list of areas to improve upon
and work on those together.
Set up a specific time to discuss problems.
Remember that you don't always have to agree—
you can agree to disagree.
Have time apart from each other.
Keep your friends.
Make a list of new activities to do on your dates.
Have other interests besides each other.
Confront each other when a problem arises,
instead of letting it fester and build.
Work at being romantic and thoughtful.

1335. Support your local Civic Theater.

1336. Tell your date about your day at work.

1337. Go sight seeing on a Sunday afternoon.

1338. Spend the date doing what your significant other wants to do, instead of what you want to do.

1339. See a movie (a great first date).

1340. Shop in a department store.

1341. Enjoy dinner at a steak house.

1342. Spend a day together at the mall.

1343. Go out for pizza.

1344. Watch one of the all time favorites, *The Wizard of Oz.*

1345. Take time out of your busy day to meet for lunch.

1346. Share all of your jokes.

1347. Prepare a home cooked meal.

1348. Follow the antics of Charlie Brown, Snoopy and the gang.

1349. Attend a Good Friday service.

1350. Browse a pet store.

1351. Celebrate the birds returning in the spring with a picnic in the park.

1352. Help her to make decisions when shopping for clothing.

With a Little Help from Your Friends

1353. Challenge other couples to a clabber tournament.

1354. Have your friends prepare and serve you two a romantic dinner.

1355. Serve up a volleyball party together.

1356. After the game, meet up with your friends for dinner.

1357. Pass on secondhand compliments.

1358. Group date.

1359. Throw a finals' week party after finals are finally over.

1360. Host a pot luck dinner.

1361. Play peacemaker among other couples having dating problems.

1362. Team up to support a fund raising event.

1363. Have a "mystery date"—a friend makes all of the arrangements.

1364. Shape up together at a Weight Watchers class.

1365. Host a roast.

It's Music to My Ears

1366. Crank up the Victrola to play your parents' old 78's.

1367. With your ear plugs, attend a rock concert.

1368. Enjoy soul music.

1369. While taking a fitness walk through the park, share a Walkman .

1370. Sing our National Anthem at a ballgame.

1371. Check out a local band.

1372. Go Christmas caroling together.

1373. Listen to new songs on the radio.

1374. Pick out your favorite tunes on a jukebox.

1375. Relax while listening to the waves crash against the shore.

1376. Share a loveseat to watch the Grammy Awards.

1377. Sing hymns.

1378. Try yodeling (but not in public).

1379. Listen to a great pianist perform.

1380. For an evening of perfect harmony, go to a barbershop quartet concert.

1381. Record your own record.

1382. Prepare for the upcoming winter by putting up a birdhouse with a feeder .

1383. For a southern flair, enjoy a Dixieland band.

1384. Join in the fun and request your favorite songs at a piano bar.

1385. Jazz your troubles away.

1386. Pick out "your" song.

1387. Share a blanket while listening to the rain fall on a tin roof.

Love Makes the World Go 'Round

1388. Enjoy yourselves under a harvest moon.

1389. Share a roll of Life Savers.

1390. Dine at a revolving restaurant and enjoy the view.

1391. Visit each other in the hospital.

1392. Take food to a shut-in.

1393. Matchmake your dateless friends.

1394. Join in the celebration at a couple's wedding shower.

1395. Tutor a child together.

1396. Ride an old time carousel.

1397. Go to a Valentine's Day dance with someone special.

1398. Visit a picturesque windmill.

1399. Volunteer yourselves to help at an animal shelter.

PLACES TO MEET MEN

High school tracks	Martial arts classes
Bicycling	Laundromats
Bowling lanes	Work-related meetings
Sporting events	Church
Fitness centers	Sports bars

1400. Brighten someone's day by visiting an orphanage.

1401. Smooch.

1402. Make it a joint effort to cheer up a friend.

1403. Snuggle while riding a Ferris wheel.

If You Have Already Tried
the First 1,403 . . .

1404. D³ date—drinks, dinner & dancing.

1405. Frolic on a playground during your lunch hour.

1406. Exchange gifts on New Year's Day .

1407. Apply for romantic license plates.

1408. Host a Sunday supper for your friends.

1409. Improve yourselves by taking a class.

1410. Be a good sport and go along to a doll show.

1411. Pen a limerick together.

1412. Have a doughnut hole breakfast before church.

1413. Set up an aquarium in your apartment.

1414. Trade baseball cards.

1415. Write an appreciation letter to your city council.

1416. Play Chinese checkers on a cold night.

1417. For an unusual outing, try a visit to a roadhouse.

1418. Experiment cooking with a wok.

1419. Browse the classifieds for hidden treasures.

1420. Organize a progressive dinner party.

1421. Watch a western.

1422. Call in your joint pledge to a telethon and challenge other couples to do the same.

1423. Throw an Alaskan gold rush party.

1424. Make your own Candid Camera show using a Camcorder on your unsuspecting friends.

1425. Talk about your favorite books.

1426. Improve your game by taking tennis lessons together.

1427. Join a sports club.

1428. Set out to break a *Guinness* record.

1429. Host a New Year's Eve bash.

1430. Celebrate the end of summer by watching the Labor Day Telethon.

1431. Attend a political debate.

1432. Donate plasma.

1433. Listen to the *Barber of Seville* (opera).

1434. Rent out a movie theater for a private, romantic showing for two.

1435. Try imported ale.

1436. Go trailblazing.

1437. Watch the Goodwill Games.

1438. Capture special moments with an instant camera.

1439. Celebrate a jubilee.

1440. Exchange your business cards to impress each other with your titles.

1441. Start a coin collection together.

1442. Kick back and enjoy a foot massage.

You'll Feel the Earth Move

1443.   Go to a ground breaking ceremony.

1444.   Attend a stock car race together.

1445.   Head to the beach for a day of bodysurfing.

1446.   Host a clam dig .

1447.   Flip over each other on a trampoline.

1448.   Pack a lunch and spend the day 4-wheeling.

1449.   Join other concerned citizens at an Earth Day party.

1450.   Turn off the lights and spend a summer evening thunderstorm watching.

1451.   For a guaranteed blast, watch a rocket launching.

1452.   Pick grapes and stomp them.

1453.   Loosen up and do the rumba.

1454.   Watch real life cowboys in action at a rodeo.

Cupid's Choice

1455.   Send each other romantic notes.

1456.   Write your initials in wet cement inside a heart.

1457.   Dance the night away cheek to cheek.

1458.   Kiss.

1459.   Celebrate your dating anniversaries.

1460.   For a date that is right on target, try archery.

1461. Fall in love all over again.

1462. Make a toast to each other.

1463. Send a picnic basket to her office with a note directing her to bring it to a romantic spot for a wonderful time.

1464. Bring your date a chocolate rose.

1465. Hold hands during a scary movie.

1466. Sit next to a roaring fire and compose love letters to each other.

1467. Share a tin of heart shaped cookies.

1468. While at the mall, split up for fifteen minutes to buy each other a fun five dollar gift.

1469. Enjoy the beauty of a sunset picnic.

1470. Have a special Valentine's Day celebration by yourselves.

We All Have to Eat Sometime

1471. Leave out milk and cookies for Santa Claus.

1472. Try an oyster bar.

1473. Fix a junk food feast.

1474. Prepare a vegetarian meal.

1475. When your luncheon plans flounder, have your own fish fry.

1476. Grocery shop together.

1477. Take off to have dinner at an airport bistro.

1478. For a little variety when dining out, try samples of each other's meal.

1479. Pig out at a pig roast.

HIGH TECH ROMANCE
Leave a romantic message on the answering machine.
Video tape a special message.
Fax a love letter.
Make a cassette of your favorite songs.
Link-up your computers.
Video tape part of your time together.
Make a computer printout of all the things
that you like about each other.

1480. Feast on a fabulous steak dinner at a "grill your own" restaurant.

1481. Take a cooking class together.

1482. Spell out a special message in your Alphabet soup.

1483. Pick up Chinese food to go.

1484. After a wonderful home cooked meal, go out for dessert.

1485. Dine at a seafood restaurant.

1486. For a change from burgers and fries, shop at a health food store.

1487. Make a feast out of "peel your own" shrimp.

Don't Knock It Until You Have Tried It

1488.   Don't be a dead fish, try a sushi bar.

1489.   For happy feet, get a pedicure for two.

1490.   Learn to hang glide.

1491.   Celebrate Victoria Day.

1492.   Explore an oriental food mart.

1493.   Rent a hearse to go to a Halloween party in style.

1494.   Walk along the beach on a winter day.

1495.   Play spades.

1496.   Browse a hobby shop to discover a shared interest.

1497.   Collect matchbooks from all of the places that you have been together.

1498.   Watch an ice hockey game.

1499.   Relax yourselves in a sauna.

1500.   Give each other a haircut.

1501.   Play black jack, the loser buys lunch.

1502.   Don't just get mad, express yourselves by writing to your senators.

1503.   Dive into an aquatic work out, play water polo.

1504.   Team up to devise that long overdue budget.

1505.   For a hot date, follow a fire truck.

1506.   Eat with chopsticks.

1507.   Use your artistic abilities while ice sculpting.

1508.   Wash your cars in the pouring rain.

1509. Start the day off with a breakfast picnic.

1510. Work on a telethon together.

1511. Make Shakespeare proud by hosting an Elizabethan party.

1512. Be adventurous and try abseiling (a form of rock climbing).

1513. Go to a smorgasbord and make little piggies out of yourselves.

1514. Head to the high seas for a day of dolphin watching.

1515. Tread lightly while sharing your political views.

1516. Infiltrate an army-navy surplus store.

1517. Try jet skiing.

1518. Attempt to brew homemade beer.

DATING TIP
The one who does the asking out does the paying.

1519. Celebrate Guy Fawkes Day.

1520. Meet for a tavern lunch on a Saturday afternoon.

1521. Give each other a facial.

1522. While out and about the town, land at an airport duty free shop for a major bargain.

1523. Create a masterpiece on canvas.

1524. Get your ears pierced together.

1525. Have a picnic in the bottom of an empty pool.

Yesteryear

1526.   Share a milkshake at a soda fountain.

1527.   Gather seashells by the seashore.

1528.   When you are very hungry, chow down at a family style restaurant.

1529.   Play checkers in a country store.

1530.   Make Christmas stockings to get ready for Santa.

1531.   Put on your overalls and go to a barn dance.

1532.   Tell ghost stories on a stormy night.

1533.   Visit in the parlor.

1534.   Feed the ducks in the park.

1535.   Discover treasures in a country store.

1536.   Go swing dancing.

1537.   Spend a rainy afternoon haylofting.

1538.   Watch a classic movie.

1539.   Go ice skating at a local rink.

1540.   Put together a 1000-piece puzzle in one night.

1541.   Attend a 4-H fair.

1542.   Join in the fun at a church picnic.

1543.   Play bingo together.

1544.   Warm up to a bonfire on the beach.

1545.   Pop popcorn for an evening in front of the television.

1546.   Enjoy the aroma while baking bread.

1547. Host a Labor Day picnic.

1548. String cranberries for your Christmas tree.

1549. On a summer's evening, load up the car and head to a drive-in movie.

1550. Visit with your family.

1551. Decorate all of the holiday cookies and cakes she bakes.

1552. Shop for beautiful homemade heirlooms at a quilt show.

1553. Bake Valentine cookies.

1554. See if time flies, when you're having fun by telling time on a sundial.

1555. Pick apples.

Courtship consists in a number of quiet attentions, not so pointed as to alarm, nor so vague as not to be understood.

—STERNE

1556. Compete at a friendly game of pinball.

1557. Swivel the afternoon away while eating at the counter.

1558. Remain celibate until you marry.

1559. Share cotton candy.

1560. Shop for garden fresh goodies at a farmer's market.

1561. Win a goldfish at the fair.

1562. Be pirates and go on a treasure hunt.

1563. Celebrate the season at a Christmas party.

1564. Shop at a Five & Dime store.

1565. Watch a Thanksgiving Day parade.

1566. After checking each one, select and chop down a Christmas tree.

1567. Enjoy a meal at a country inn.

1568. Try candle making together.

1569. Go to a barbecue.

1570. Share an ice cold watermelon on a hot summer day.

Making Great Memories

1571. Play hooky together.

1572. Look through your high school yearbook and share memories.

1573. Write a review of your last date as if you were both famous critics.

1574. Get lost on purpose and enjoy the adventure.

1575. Celebrate a church homecoming.

1576. Rent a video camera to record the highlights of your date.

1577. Work together in a darkroom and see what develops.

1578. Visit your alma mater.

1579. Start a scrapbook of your dates together.

1580. Have your caricatures sketched by a street artist.

1581. Share the excitement of your first kiss.

1582. Invent your own holiday.

1583. Bake Christmas goodies together to give as gifts.

1584. Visit with your grandparents.

1585. Team up to play an elaborate practical joke on a good natured friend.

1586. Worship together at a Christmas Eve service.

1587. Dress up in costumes to have your picture taken at a custom photo booth.

1588. Stroll through your old neighborhood together.

Hobnobbing

1589. Meet for happy hour with friends.

1590. Enjoy yourselves while dining at the club.

1591. Rent an expensive sports car and drive by your friends' houses.

1592. Start a fan club together.

1593. Hang out at the Student Union with the gang on a Saturday afternoon.

1594. Enjoy a fine meal at a yacht club.

1595. Go to a chili dinner at school.

1596. Rent an RV to tailgate in style.

1597. Write to your favorite celebrity.

1598. Host a wine and cheese party.

1599. Hoof it to an Elk's Club dance.

1600. Meet up with your co-workers for an evening.

1601. Start the day off with a champagne breakfast.

Time-Proven Winners

1602. Make a late night junk food run.

1603. Mingle with your old friends and make new ones at a party.

1604. Treat your date to their favorite dinner.

1605. Observe Memorial Day together by laying wreaths on the graves of your loved ones and sharing fond memories.

1606. Date by cellular phone when you are both headed in different directions.

1607. Enjoy a romantic sunrise walk on the beach.

1608. Be chocoholics together.

1609. Buy a lottery ticket and dream.

1610. Join in the excitement at a professional football game.

1611. Try a basic date—go out for pizza and beer.

1612. Celebrate a red letter day.

1613. Break out of your winter doldrums by going to a Super Bowl party.

1614. Share Reeses's Pieces.

1615. Putter around all day long together.

1616. Read *Garfield.*

THE CASE AGAINST SINGLES BARS
Often too loud to talk.
Lying abounds.
Many are looking for a one night stand.
Not everyone is single.
Can be expensive.
Peer pressure.
A lot of game playing.
"Plastic" people.
Can be very depressing.
Emotionally draining if done frequently.

1617. After a deep freeze, go ice skating outdoors.

1618. Throw a gala party .

1619. Go out for a steak dinner.

1620. Host a Halloween party.

1621. Attempt to win a prize at the carnival.

1622. Videotape your date playing sports.

1623. Share Oreo cookies and milk after a long day.

1624. Discuss current events.

1625. Watch the Westminster Dog Show.

1626. Take it easy while celebrating Labor Day.

1627. Volunteer to be the designated driver.

1628. Fix a snack together.

1629. Spend the day at a theme park.

1630. View a touring exhibit at the museum.

1631. Join in the excitement of a ticker-tape parade.

1632. Watch a late night talk show for a laugh.

1633. Share your best travel stories.

1634. Enjoy a quick meal at a fast food restaurant.

1635. For a laugh, read the *Weekly World News.*

1636. Write a personal ad for a single friend.

1637. Bake Toll House cookies.

1638. Celebrate July 4th by creating some fireworks of your own.

1639. Share expenses on a Dutch treat date.

1640. Go nightclubbing.

1641. Make chili on a cold night.

1642. Amuse yourselves at an amusement park.

1643. Invite your friends over for a quiet evening.

1644. Relax at the beach.

1645. Treat yourselves to a Dairy Queen Blizzard.

1646. Watch a professional tennis match.

1647. Make tacos for your pals.

1648. Share your daily events.

1649. Hang out with happily married couples.

1650. Join the crowd at a New Year's Eve party.

Learning Can Be Fun

1651. Spend a quiet afternoon together in the library.

1652. Play along with a television game show.

1653. Cure your "hunt and peck" method by taking a typing class together.

1654. Share your expertise by tutoring each other.

1655. Grab a blanket and study on the lawn.

1656. Teach each other the intricacies of your favorite sport.

1657. Learn about yourselves at a handwriting analyst.

1658. Get the facts straight by reading the *Almanac* together.

1659. Tackle a project from a "how to" book.

1660. Get in the swing of things by taking golf lessons.

1661. Volunteer to teach Vacation Bible School.

1662. Read *2002 Answers to Compatibility Questions.*

1663. Teach your old dog new tricks.

1664. Take keyboard lessons together.

1665. Help each other write computer programs.

Shop 'Til You Drop

1666. Buy decorations the day after Christmas for half price.

1667. The lazy way to shop—thumb through a Sear's catalog together.

1668. Browse the video store for a movie to rent.

1669. Check out a library book sale.

1670. Go apartment hunting.

1671. Hunt for goodies at a church bazaar.

1672. Team up to haggle for the best price from a street vendor.

1673. Search for a good buy at a thrift shop.

1674. Sort through the junk at a yard sale.

1675. Go to a pet store to fetch home unique toys for your pet.

1676. Browse an L.L. Bean catalog.

1677. Instead of fighting the mall traffic, stay at home to shop by phone.

1678. Help her pick out her perfume.

1679. Help him pick out his cologne.

1680. Catch your breath and grab a bite to eat at the mall food court.

1681. Clip Sunday coupons for future savings.

1682. Buy matching watches.

1683. Go menu shopping in a restaurant district.

Pleased to Meet You

1684. Introduce your date to your best friend.

1685. Collect autographs together.

1686. Meet for cocktails with a sibling.

1687. Tell Santa what you want for Christmas.

1688. Watch an Elvis impersonator.

1689. Tell humorous family stories.

1690. Visit a wax museum.

1691. Meet her sorority sisters.

1692. Meet his fraternity brothers.

1693. Tell tales about your co-workers.

1694. Introduce your boss to your date.

1695. Look through your college yearbook.

1696. Trace your family trees to uncover any nobility.

1697. Have your date meet your pet.

1698. Introduce your date to your parents.

1699. Write your date's personal history.

1700. Go backstage after a concert.

Celebrate

1701. Exchange a small gift on St. Nicholas night.

1702. Join in the fun of a couple's baby shower.

1703. Observe Martin Luther King Day.

1704. Turn Flag Day into a gala event by having a huge party.

1705. Attend a Lenten service together.

1706. Go to a July 4th picnic.

1707. Pass out candy cigars after your dog has puppies or your cat has kittens.

1708. Gather with old friends at a college reunion.

REASONS FOR YOU TO ENTERTAIN
It's great fun.
It can give an occasion a more special feeling.
You'll get a return invitation.
It could rekindle an old flame or spark a new one.
It is a neat way to say thanks for a special night out.
People like being invited.
It is a way to impress your date.
It provides a relaxed atmosphere to learn
more about another person.
It is a super way to meet new people.

1709. Celebrate Mardi Gras by dressing up in fun costumes and inviting your pals over for some Cajun food.

1710. Enjoy a full moon.

1711. Savor the longest day of the year by pausing to take stock of your relationship.

1712. Celebrate the Twelve Days of Christmas.

1713. Go out for an anniversary dinner.

1714. Show your pride by flying the flag.

1715. Frolic in the first snowfall of the year.

1716. Toast the Irish with a green beer.

Do You Like to . . .

1717. Solve the Sunday crossword puzzle together.

1718. Visit a masseuse to unwind.

1719. Share a stromboli.

1720. Watch boats on a river.

1721. Exercise together to shed a few pounds.

1722. Enjoy cappuccino and conversation.

1723. Try Latin dancing.

1724. Be a sport and watch bowl games all day long on January 1st.

1725. Make a frozen strawberry daiquiri.

1726. Create a work of art with a paint-by-numbers kit.

1727. Watch a field hockey game.

1728. Round-up another couple to shop at a western apparel store.

1729. Be brave and try oysters on the half shell.

1730. Buckle up and take off on a three-wheeler adventure.

1731. Take a walking tour of your city.

1732. Listen to some rap music.

1733. Spice up your evening by dining at a Mexican restaurant.

1734. Do brass etchings together.

1735. Explore a trade show.

1736. Gather with friends to play Uno.

1737. Create your own special blend of spiced tea.

1738. Lace up your sneakers and play a game of basketball.

1739. Rent mopeds for the day.

1740. Discover reggae music.

1741. Visit an orchard.

1742. Attend an awards banquet.

That's Show Business

1743. Watch an Agatha Christie movie and try to figure out whodunit.

1744. Combine your talents and participate in a talent show.

1745. After dark, watch the stars come out when hosting a Hollywood party.

1746. Get on television by doing something outrageous.

1747. Experience life at a cabaret.

1748. Enter your four legged buddy in a dog show.

1749. Audition for a part in a play together.

1750. Thumb through *Leonard Maltin's TV Movies & Video Guide* to find something good to watch.

1751. Be adventurous and try experimental theater.

1752. Watch a mime artist perform.

1753. Check out a sneak preview.

1754. When you can't make it to Broadway, go see a local play.

1755. Make a list of your top five movies of all time.

1756. After the show, host a cast party.

1757. Participate in community theater together.

1758. Do your own movie review while driving home from the cinema.

1759. Be daring and perform at a Karaoke Club.

Faint heart never won fair lady.
—CERVANTES

When in Rome . . .

New York City

1760. Capture the flavor of the city by street noshing.

1761. Expand your horizons from the top of the World Trade Center.

1762. Sample the tastes and sounds of Little Italy.

1763. Join trendsetters from all over the world at Bloomingdale's.

San Francisco

1764. Break out and tour Alcatraz.

1765. Tour Sausalito on a sunny day.

1766. Be awed in the redwood country.

1767. Saunter through Union Square for fabulous shopping.

1768. On a Sunday afternoon, join the crowd at the Golden Gate Park.

St. Louis

1769. Head for "The Hill" for the best Italian food this side of Rome.

1770. Lift your spirits atop the Gateway Arch.

1771. Shop Plaza Frontenac—the midwest's answer to Rodeo Drive .

1772. Stroll through the Central West End.

1773. Spend a delightful evening under the stars at the Muny.

Indianapolis

1774. Enjoy the beauty of Brown County in the fall.

1775. Feel like a child again as you tour the Children's Museum.

1776. Race to the Indianapolis Motor Speedway for a tour.

Denver

1777. Shop the day away at Larimer Square.

1778. Watch the Broncos play at the famous Mile High Stadium.

1779. Treat yourselves to one of the free summertime outdoor symphony concerts.

1780. If you are short on cash, try a visit to the Denver Mint.

Dallas

1781. Get on over to the Mesquite Championship Rodeo.

1782. Fight the massive crowd at the Texas State Fair.

1783. Get up early to check out the goods at the Farmers' Market.

1784. Check out JR's spread at Southfork Ranch.

1785. For an international flavor, try sipping tea while watching a cricket match at the Dallas Cricket Club.

Nashville

1786. Indulge yourselves with a fabulous weekend brunch at the Opryland Hotel.

1787. Fiddle the day away on Music Row.

1788. Hop aboard a riverboat replica for a cruise on the Cumberland River.

1789. Visit the Hermitage to catch a glimpse of the Old South.

New Orleans

1790. Enjoy the beauty and charm of the beautiful mansions in the Garden District.

1791. Be entertained with a walk through the French Quarter.

1792. If you like big parties, delight in the festivities of Mardi Gras.

1793. Hunt for hidden artist's treasures along Jackson Square.

Los Angeles

1794. Watch your step at Mann's Chinese Theater.

1795. Discover all there is to do at Venice Beach.

1796. For a taste of "Olde England" try the Renaissance Pleasure Faires.

1797. Get away for the day on Catalina Island.

Welcome to My Abode

1798. Show off your new place by hosting an apartment warming party.

1799. Spend the day on a houseboat.

1800. After a big party, be a good sport and help clean the carpet.

1801. Shop for a housewarming gift for a friend.

1802. Help hang wallpaper.

1803. Host an open house during the holidays.

1804. The perfect yuppie date—go condo hunting.

1805. Hang pictures together and get them even for a change.

1806. Help him decorate his bachelor pad.

1807. Ask your date to help you bargain shop for major appliances.

1808. Build an unusual doghouse (Fido will love this).

1809. Enjoy TV dinners in front of the tube.

1810. Go furniture shopping.

1811. Check out several house auctions for a real estate bargain.

1812. Help rearrange her apartment.

SIGNS THAT YOUR RELATIONSHIP
HAS A FUTURE
You enjoy each other.
You plan future dates together.
You feel mutually committed to the relationship.
Your friends consider you a couple.
You see each other on a regular basis.
You can be yourselves around each other.
You look forward to spending time together.

1813. Gather ideas at a Home Show.

1814. Team up to tackle the never ending list of things to fix around the house.

1815. Put on old clothes to paint your place.

Life in the Fast Lane

1816. For wintertime excitement, go snowmobiling.

1817. Learn to ride a skateboard together.

1818. Rent a golf cart to go for a different kind of Sunday drive.

WHAT NOT TO DO ON FIRST DATES
Talk only about yourself.
Be late.
Compare your present date to past dates.
Flirt with others.
Tell your life story including private details.
Ask your date extremely personal questions.
Dress in an inappropriate manner.
Be a complainer.
Brag.
Order food which is difficult to eat.
Go somewhere that you aren't comfortable.
Make the date too long.
Be "too nice."

1819. Team up in a wheelbarrow race.

1820. Take driving lessons together.

1821. Take a gamble and spend the evening at a casino.

1822. Gallop off to a derby party.

1823. Enter a three-legged race together at a picnic.

1824. Split a bottle of champagne.

1825. Hold hands and scream during a roller coaster ride.

1826. Get around Chinatown in a rickshaw.

1827. Don't blink or you might miss the action at a hot rod race.

1828. Enjoy the fast track while racing slot cars.

1829. Soak up the rays while you enjoy the day at a regatta.

1830. Chase down an ice cream truck.

1831. Gentlemen (and ladies), start your summer fun at an Indy 500 party.

1832. Go barhopping together.

1833. Challenge each other to a pogo stick race.

1834. Race off to a track meet.

1835. Try an exhilarating giant slide ride.

1836. Watch a kayak race.

1837. Head off into the wild blue yonder after taking flying lessons together.

1838. Test drive expensive sports cars.

1839. Hold on tight while bobsledding.

1840. Cover your ears during the thunder of a hydroplane race.

1841. The perfect workout: put on your sweat suit and running shoes, turn on the television, sit on the couch and watch the Boston Marathon.

1842. Get out of town to watch a cross country road rally.

1843. Race go-karts at an amusement park (the loser gets a chance to get even at bumper cars).

Who Said that Three's a Crowd?

1844. Visit a maternity ward together to see a friend's baby.

1845. Bring your dog along on a picnic.

1846. Spend a day in the park taking pictures of your pet.

1847. Drop in on old friends.

1848. Take your cat to the vet.

1849. Have a fun evening babysitting together.

1850. Dress your dog in a costume for a special outing.

1851. Invite a friend along for an evening out.

1852. Take your cat with you to a drive-in movie.

1853. Adopt a pet and name it after your date.

1854. Pet sit together.

1855. Invite your minister along to lunch.

1856. Play frisbee with your dog in the park.

Express Yourselves

1857. Give each other a nickname.

1858. Be creative and compose your own song.

1859. Try saying tongue twisters.

1860. Speak in a funny diction for the entire date.

1861. Say grace.

1862. Challenge each other at word games.

1863. Exercise your constitutional rights by voting.

1864. Share part of your diary.

1865. Dress up as your hero and heroine and go to a costume party.

1866. Have a fax date.

1867. Amuse yourselves with a game of Scrabble.

1868. Write a letter to Santa.

1869. Read to each other on a lazy spring afternoon.

1870. Spend a Saturday morning painting clown faces at a home for underprivileged children.

1871. Put a note in a bottle and set it adrift in the sea.

1872. Take a sculpting class together.

1873. Draw pictures in the sand.

1874. Set off fireworks on your dating anniversaries.

1875. Volunteer to work together one night a week at a Crisis Line.

1876. Make a fun prank phone call to a friend.

1877. Speak your mind by writing a letter to the editor.

1878. Get published (we did).

1879. Copyright something (we did that, too).

1880. Meet for a quick cup of espresso before work on a winter's morning.

Little Things Mean a Lot

1881. Go out on the town to celebrate your new job.

1882. Share a blanket on a cold night at a football game.

1883. Nurse your date back to health when illness strikes.

1884. Make greeting cards together for your friends.

1885. Eat crow when necessary.

1886. Gift wrap presents by wrapping items in many boxes tucked inside of each other.

1887. Be a sport and rub Ben Gay on sore aching muscles.

1888. Visit a cemetery together to lend support.

1889. Enjoy being comfortable enough that you don't feel like you must talk all of the time.

1890. Cure each other of the hiccups.

1891. Buy Girl Scout cookies and share them.

1892. During a tough time, go out of your way to cheer each other up.

1893. Visit a friend in the hospital.

1894. Surprise her with a ride home from work.

1895. Make your date's birthday a festive occasion.

1896. When the flu season hits, chauffeur each other to the doctor's office.

1897. Team up to take your dog to the veterinarian.

1898. Display yellow ribbons to support our overseas troops.

1899. Surprise each other with a bottle of wine.

1900. Host a sympathy party for a friend who has just split up with their significant other.

1901. Deliver Christmas gifts together to friends.

1902. Drop by the office and have an impromptu date.

1903. Have the unending patience to teach your date how to water ski on one ski.

Food & Spirits

1904. Browse a cheese shop for munchies for your television night at home.

1905. Roast chestnuts during the holidays.

1906. With two juicy steaks in hand, go to a cook out party.

1907. Enjoy the aroma of a bakery while the two of you pick out dessert for dinner.

1908. Stroll through a vineyard.

1909. Shop a liquor store for the ingredients to create an exotic drink.

1910. Take a wine appreciation class together.

1911. For a different evening, host a fondue party for your friends.

1912. Cook the entire meal in the fireplace.

1913. Imagine that both of you are in the islands while sipping a pina colada.

1914. Treat yourselves to an ice cream sundae on a Sunday.

1915. Prepare a flaming dish without setting the house on fire.

1916. Browse a gourmet food shop.

1917. Team up to enter an Oreo stacking contest.

1918. Prepare an exotic ethnic dinner.

1919. Make homemade wine.

1920. Bake a birthday cake together for someone special.

1921. Tour a brewery on a Saturday afternoon.

1922. Make a late night doughnut run.

Recreation Means Fun and Adventure

1923. Experience the thrill of an ultralight plane ride.

1924. Try lawn bowling.

1925. Sharpen your game at a driving range.

1926. Enjoy a spring afternoon row boating.

1927. Kick off your shoes to play sand volleyball.

1928. Sail away.

1929. Hit the links for a round of par 3 golf.

1930. Go windsurfing.

1931. On coed night, work out together at the gym.

1932. Take a Sunday afternoon bike ride.

1933. Go rainbow watching after a storm.

1934. Skim through your day on an air boat.

1935. Shape up together at a health spa.

Toward a Perfect Relationship

1936. Take a compatibility test.

1937. Compare lists of traits you'd like to improve.

1938. Throw away your old black books.

GIFTS TO IMPRESS
Sterling silver picture frame with a
picture of the two of you.
Antique quilt for bundling up on cold nights.
Fine chocolates.
Orchids.
Pearls.
Cashmere muffler and sweaters.
Antique jewelry.
Gold cuff links.
Locket with your picture.

1939. Share your pet peeves.

1940. Celebrate Leap Year on February 29th.

1941. Worship together outside of church.

1942. Kiss and make up after a fight.

1943. Hold a brainstorm session on how to improve your relationship.

1944. Be a true friend to each other during a tough time.

1945. Play "shrink" to help overcome a problem.

1946. Reveal any previously told white lies.

1947. Improve yourselves at a self esteem seminar.

1948. Celebrate your 25th, 50th, etc., dates.

1949. Pray for each other.

1950. Admit your quirks (but not too many at one time).

1951. Share breath mints after eating pizza.

1952. Take the day off to cure spring fever.

1953. Always keep your word to each other.

Take the High Road

1954. Be chauffeured around town in a stretch limousine.

1955. Celebrate All Saints Day on November 1st by being extra nice to each other.

1956. Celebrate Easter together.

1957. Stroll hand in hand along a levee.

1958. Share your religious beliefs.

1959. For a fond farewell, take your date to the airport.

1960. Attend a Sunday school class together.

1961. Create a front yard work of art by making snow angels.

1962. Experience a back road jeep ride.

1963. When you are snowed in, watch a church service on television.

1964. Visit a local mission to lend your support.

1965. Sing in the church choir together.

1966. Take communion together.

1967. Attend a friend's baby christening.

1968. Slow down from life's fast pace by fasting together .

1969. Browse a religious bookstore.

1970. Visit a live nativity scene to help experience the real meaning of Christmas.

1971. Enjoy a rooftop picnic.

1972. Observe the Sabbath.

1973. Attend a church service and then go out for a special lunch.

1974. Tour the historical churches in your area.

Our Favorites

1975. Read the Bible together.

1976. Enjoy an all American picnic—hot dogs, chips, and apple pie.

1977. Share a recliner to watch a scary movie.

1978. Put on your crash helmets to battle it out in bumper cars.

1979. Have a party for your dog upon graduation from obedience school.

1980. Sail away in a catamaran.

1981. Carry mistletoe and use it.

1982. Drive around on a December night to enjoy the Christmas lights.

1983. Celebrate Hump Day (Wednesday).

1984. Go to the best deli in town to order the biggest sandwich they have and split it.

1985. Kick off your holiday celebration by dyeing Easter eggs.

1986. Go to a teddy bear convention.

1987. Be adventurous and try something absolutely, positively, and entirely new.

1988. Nibble the ears off a chocolate Easter bunny.

1989. Have a squirt gun fight.

1990. See all of the movies that were nominated for Academy Awards this year.

1991. Create a photo montage of your dates together.

1992. Treat each other to a back massage.

1993. Experience a scenic chair lift ride.

1994. Attend the Special Olympics.

1995. Conserve cash by enjoying the free things in life.

1996. Share a hammock on a summer day.

1997. When the rain interrupts your plans, have an impromptu picnic in the car.

1998. Fritter the day away together.

1999. Satisfy your sweet tooth by making a meal entirely from the pastry tray at a fine restaurant.

2000. Enjoy the hustle and bustle of the holiday season.

2001. Spend the day floating side by side in a pool.

2002. READ THIS BOOK TOGETHER!

ALSO BY CYNDI HAYNES & DALE EDWARDS

2002 Romantic Ideas
$5.95, 144 pages
ISBN 1-55850-819-8

2002 Ways to Find, Attract, and Keep a Mate
$5.95, 144 pages
ISBN 1-58062-081-7

2002 Ways to Say "I Love You"
$5.95, 144 pages
1-58062-080-9

Available Wherever Books Are Sold

If you cannot find these titles at your favorite retail outlet, you may order them directly from the publisher. BY PHONE: Call 1-800-872-5627. We accept Visa, Mastercard, and American Express. $4.95 will be added to your total order for shipping and handling. BY MAIL: Write out the full titles of the books you'd like to order and send payment, including $4.95 for shipping and handling, to: Adams Media Corporation, 260 Center Street, Holbrook, MA 02343. 30-day money-back guarantee.